LEADING A
SPECIAL
NEEDS
MINISTRY

AMY FENTON LEE

LEADING A
SPECIAL
NEEDS
MINISTRY

A PRACTICAL GUIDE TO INCLUDING **CHILDREN & LOVING FAMILIES**

B&H
PUBLISHING GROUP
NASHVILLE, TENNESSEE

978-1-4336-4712-3

Published by B&H Publishing Group
Nashville, Tennessee

First Edition 2013

Dewey Decimal Classification: 259.4
Subject Heading: SPECIAL NEEDS MINISTRY \ CHURCH WORK
WITH PEOPLE WITH DISABILITIES \ HANDICAPPED

1 2 3 4 5 6 7 • 20 19 18 17 16

To Watson:

Your creativity, humor, and compassion
are evidence of God's beautiful handiwork.

To Brian:

Thank you for being my "benefactor" before anyone
else believed in what I was doing.

To Dad:

Thanks for bravely taking a very talkative and inquisitive little girl
along with you on hospital and nursing home visits to church
members. It was a gift to grow comfortable in these settings and
more importantly, to learn to look for the stories in those encounters.
Most of all, thanks for being a great mentor for the last four decades.

CONTENTS

Acknowledgments   ix

Section 1: Loving Families

1. Loving the Family through the Diagnosis: At-Birth Diagnosis   5

2. Loving the Family through the Diagnosis: Neurological-Related
   Diagnosis in Preschool or Elementary School Years   18

Section 2: A Practical Guide to Including Children

3. Special Needs Statistics, Terms, Laws, and Trends   39

4. Establishing a Mission for the Special Needs Ministry   49

5. Developing an Accommodation Plan for the Child with
   Special Needs   61

6. The Special Needs Ministry Leader   86

7. Volunteers: Leading, Recruiting, Training, and Creating
   Community   102

8. Behavior and Participant Safety   122

9. FAQs (Frequently Asked Questions)   140

10. Including Teens with Special Needs   156

Appendix 1.1: Tips for Loving the Family Through the Diagnosis   171

Appendix 1.2: Give Disability Visibility   172

Appendix 7.1: Policies and Volunteer Training Topics   174

Appendix 7.2: Teen Volunteer Training Event   188

Appendix 7.3: Church Greeter/Host Training Events   194

Appendix 7.4: Volunteer Opportunities Other Than Childcare   198

Appendix 8.1: Inclusion Tips and Behavior Management Strategies   200

Notes   205

About the Author   209

ACKNOWLEDGMENTS

Special thanks to my friends at LifeWay and Broadman & Holman. This group rallied behind this book, working at supersonic speed to make the resource available again. In addition, I will be forever grateful to **Steve Laube**, my stellar agent, who rolled up his sleeves when he took me on as a client. I have benefitted tremendously from his shepherding.

I owe gratitude to three individuals in particular for their help with this resource. Prior to my personal remarks and for the benefit of the reader, I have included a professional bio for each of these contributors. While I do not hold formal academic credentials in the area of my own expertise, I am proud to say this book has been shaped and reviewed by respected voices that do hold such credentials.

Dr. Alyssa Barnes

Alyssa Barnes has a passion for children with special needs and seeing them included with their typical peers. She holds a Bachelor of Science of Education in early childhood/elementary education from Samford University, a Master of Education from the University of Virginia, and a Doctor of Philosophy from the University of Georgia, both in special education. Dr. Barnes has taught in elementary school-aged inclusion environments for school districts across the Atlanta, GA metro area. Recently Dr. Barnes served as assistant professor in the Early Childhood/Special Education Program at the University of North Georgia. Dr. Barnes founded the All Children's Playground Project at Centennial Olympic Park. This facility opened in 2008 to provide children with special needs the opportunity to play alongside typically developing peers. Alyssa is a lifelong member of Marietta First United Methodist Church.

Dr. Barnes has been more than gracious with her time and knowledge for the past nine years, giving interviews and reviewing a countless number of my earlier writings. She has also answered questions when unique dilemmas would arise with a church in network of connections. Her expertise in public policy, national trends, and special education law has been invaluable. And this book is a better book thanks to Dr. Barnes's consultative review.

Katie Garvert

Katie is running on all cylinders when she is collaborating with a church staff, helping them develop a vision for including individuals with disabilities. Her consulting work with church leaders was born out of a decade of ministry leadership and her ongoing work as an educator in the Colorado public school system. Until 2014 and for nine years, Katie led Woodman Valley Chapel's Access Ministries, establishing innovative inclusion programming across the church's multiple Colorado Springs campuses. During her tenure, the disability ministry launched regular respite events, a support group for fathers, sibling retreats, and a unique overnight camp experience for students with special needs. Katie developed strong bonds with the nearly 100 Access Ministries families, frequently serving as their advocate in school meetings and connecting them with various local agencies. In 2014, Katie's family relocated to the Colorado Mountains, prompting her return to her roots as a special education teacher. Currently Katie instructs and advocates for teens with invisible disabilities at Summit High School in Frisco, Colorado. I am especially indebted to Katie for much of the content in chapter 10, which came from interviews on my website.

As a ministry leader who has encountered virtually every type of special needs situation in the context of the church, Katie's insight has given me the vehicle for translating the theoretical to the practical. So much of my ability to ask questions and develop ideas around this subject matter is the result of Katie's investment in me.

Cara Martens

Cara has a varied background in education and ministry. She holds certifications in and has taught Special Education in the public schools—inclusion, resource, and self-contained—as well as teaching in regular elementary and preschool settings. Cara also served on staff at her church as the early childhood and family experiences director. More recently, Cara served as writer and curriculum director for the reThink Group. Cara lives in Flower Mound, Texas, along with her husband and young children.

Cara is one of the most well-read individuals I've ever encountered. Her ability to connect ideas and insights from two seemingly unrelated subject matters is brilliant. And her editorial eye and ideas throughout this manuscript made it a better, more interesting read.

———

Finally, I owe thanks to many unnamed people who provided me hours and hours of interviews over the last decade. When I was writing the early drafts of this manuscript I intended to name everyone but quickly realized that a proper acknowledgments section would be a chapter in and of itself. Many church leaders and ministry volunteers have granted me lengthy, in-depth interviews as well as tours of church space. Many of these same people have responded to emails and calls at all hours of the day, helping me with this manuscript and countless other projects. To those people (and you know who you are): thanks for your time and energy around this subject matter. This book would not have been possible without each of you.

Section 1

Loving Families

Loving Families

Several years ago, I wrote two articles for a Christian publication that targets adult female readers. I offered relational etiquette for comforting a peer in the midst of grief. For the purposes of the articles, grief was described in broad terms, including difficult life changes in addition to death. We received quite a bit of feedback.

Some readers shared that they had been the friend who said all the wrong things. Other readers said that they were the person who experienced the difficult event and suffered in isolation. Shortly after one article was published, the editor suggested that I pen a similar piece, but this time offer guidance for support of mothers of children with special needs. The topic had been on the editor's heart and mine too. We both wanted to encourage the average person to do a better job of engaging her neighbors, sisters, and friends who were parenting a child with a disability. I readily accepted the editor's challenge and began researching for the assigned article.

The source of the greatest relational bruising for these parents had been the church.

What started out as plan to interview a handful of mothers who had a child with a disability, ultimately exploded into a much bigger project—interviews with more than sixty mothers of children with special needs. The following weeks would shape the rest of my life.

3

It was evident from the early interviews that these mothers were hungry for someone to engage them, to ask about their children, and to care about their own emotional health. These mothers were repeatedly conveying a deep sense of loneliness and grief. And I learned something I was not altogether prepared to hear. I discovered that by and large, the source of the greatest relational bruising for these parents had been the *church*.

In the midst of the research, I decided to make arrangements to attend a church-sponsored support group for mothers of children with special needs. The gracious ministry leader who regularly moderated the group discussions gave me the floor the entire night. I posed the same questions I had asked in the individual interviews. For three hours, I listened to variations of remarkably similar stories from probably two dozen women attending the group. Feeling tired and teary-eyed as I pulled out of that church parking lot late that night, I knew I wanted to refocus my writing to change what was being said and felt by so many. My desire was for the next wave of mothers to tell stories of comfort, connection, and renewal when they recounted their church experiences. Perhaps the people of the church could provide a spiritual oasis in the midst of an otherwise chaotic life.

When I sat down to actually write the assigned article, I sifted through my notes from the individual interviews and the night at the support group. I looked for solutions, examples of when something went right with Christian friends, and tangible pointers that church leaders could gain from my interviews. And I just started writing. I've been writing articles on various related topics ever since, now, many years later.

While the material that follows is the product of approximately sixty initial interviews with mothers, it has been critiqued in detail and influenced by several fathers of a child with special needs as well. This final draft also takes into account multiple reviews by parents not involved in the original interviews. In addition, the material here has been affirmed and sometimes refined after leading workshops at ministry conferences and similar writing on my own blog, at www.theinclusivechurch.com.

It is my hope that the guidance provided here will equip the church to support the family of a child with special needs.

1. Loving the Family through the Diagnosis: At-Birth Diagnosis

Friends, small group leaders, and church staff quickly rush to the aid of families experiencing most major life crises. Calls and casseroles—yes, I'm from the South—are common gestures of concern and support during times of birth, illness, and loss. Yet, when it comes to supporting parents who are wading through the emotional quicksand of their child's initial special needs diagnosis, it can be a struggle to find the words to reach out in the right way. Sometimes, even Christians say the wrong thing at the wrong time. I confess I have been guilty of this myself. Sadly, after the wrong thing is done or said by someone who is well intentioned, parents who have a child with special needs still suffer in silence and isolation, without feeling the support of a larger family of faith.

I believe that can change. I have witnessed the support, encouragement, and care provided by an effective ministry to children with special needs and their families. My desire is to equip you with the knowledge I've gained after interviewing dozens of mothers of children with special needs. This knowledge, paired with the practical directions that I include, will help you confidently engage and support families impacted by disability.

Throughout this section, I have interjected relational etiquette true and false questions that I pose
to audience members when I teach a workshop
from this material. These questions may be helpful
to use in a training event for volunteers.

As is the case with any life-changing disappointment, how a family processes a special needs diagnosis is always unique and personal. However,
after conducting numerous in-depth interviews with parents of children
with special needs, common themes and markers did surface for how church
staff members and lay ministers might effectively support these families. In
the course of listening to many parent stories facing these circumstances,
two predominant types of situations emerged. Each type requires ministry
teams to take slightly different approaches:

1. A family discovers a special needs diagnosis suddenly and usually
    in *close proximity to the birth of the child.* The problems may
    be revealed during prenatal testing, at the birth of the child, or
    shortly thereafter. Examples of this scenario would be giving birth
    to a child with Down syndrome, a chromosomal abnormality, or
    significant physical birth defect.

2. Through a *slower process of discovery,* a child receives a neurolog-
    ical-related special needs diagnosis during the toddler, preschool, or
    early grade-school years. Examples of this type of diagnosis include
    autism spectrum disorder, Asperger syndrome, or moderate to
    profound cases of various learning disabilities or behavior health
    disorders.

While no one approach should be applied to every family facing similar
challenges, guidelines for ministry to each type of diagnosis will be covered.
For the remainder of this chapter, we will address the at-birth diagnosis.
Aspects of discovering a child's disability through a slower process will be
addressed in chapter 2.

Assign a First Responder on a Case-by-Case Basis

As word spreads that a family may be in the midst of receiving a lifelong diagnosis for their child, assign a single person from the church to reach out, stay in contact, and assess the ongoing needs of the family. This person will be the designated *first responder*. If possible, select someone with an existing relationship with the parents. For example, avoid sending the preschool minister to the parents if that staff person has not interacted previously with the couple. Rather, a staff person who has an established rapport will likely provide a more authentic and meaningful encounter with the parents. Even better, the lay leader from the couple's small group or Sunday morning fellowship group may serve as the best first responder.

> The most valued first encounters are typically initiated by someone with whom the parents are already comfortable.

While there may be individuals on the staff with more professional knowledge related to the diagnosis, or with greater experience handling families in crises, the most valued first encounters are typically initiated by someone with whom the parents are already comfortable. In churches with cradle-care or expectant-parent ministries,[1] relationships and protocols may already exist for handling these foreseen situations. Keep in mind that the current generation of young parents desires an authentic, "we-are-in-this-with-you," type of relationship. Receiving interest from a perceived peer is more welcome than a call from an unknown staff member functioning in an obligatory, pastoral-care role.

In virtually every situation, there eventually will be an appropriate time for less familiar church staff members to engage and support the parents. How and when this will happen is best determined after an initial contact is made by the first responder, after the family's needs are assessed.

Relational Etiquette Question #1
T/F—Only place the family facing a diagnosis of a special needs nature on church prayer lists after permission has been given by parents.
Answer: True

Over the course of interviews, it was revealed that families had vastly different preferences regarding personal privacy. Some parents—and often one parent more than the other—yearned for public support during and after the child's diagnosis. These families recounted their appreciation for a visible outpouring of interest from their extended church family. They talked about the comfort and assurance they experienced because of the concern shown by small group leaders, staff members, and other church acquaintances.

However, other parents were intensely private and not ready for everyone to know about their child's diagnosis. Because preferences in these matters vary widely, the first and most important job of the first responder is to assess the family's privacy values. It is imperative that the family's explicit permission be obtained before sharing details about their family situation in a staff meeting, on prayer lists, or on posts to social media.

Relational Etiquette Question #2
T/F—Assure the family that the church will love and accept their child as God created him or her.
Answer: True

While privacy may be a central concern, for those individuals who have permission to know about the family's situation, it is important to convey their love and acceptance of the child. Nearly every interviewed mother shared that hearing the words, "Your child is loved and welcomed here," could not come soon enough. Most parents experience anxiety over whether or not the church will accept and accommodate their child with special needs. Early interactions with families can be opportunities for staff leaders to ease parents' fears, assuring them of the child's great worth in God's sight and in the church's as well. This is also the time to convey the church's intent to accommodate any unique needs the child and family may have.

Relational Etiquette Question #3
T/F—In-person contact is best for church members wanting to support parents of a newborn with a special needs diagnosis.
Answer: False

Utilize Emails and Texts for First Contact

Many parents recall moments of unexpected grief in the early days after receiving their child's diagnosis. And some parents felt embarrassment for the severity of their personal feelings of grief. During interviews, families revealed they appreciated emails, texts, and voicemail messages as the first means of contact from church staff and friends who wanted to express concern. While these methods of communication might seem impersonal, they actually give parents the ability to choose to whom, how, and when they would respond, significantly lowering the parents' stress. Impromptu home or hospital visits were less convenient for the families. Several mothers recounted stories of feeling the need to host a visitor, often a church staff member, who showed up while the family was dealing with a difficult medical issue or even working through an unexpected wave of intense emotion. Parents also shared the desire to maintain their dignity and converse with composure. This was especially true of fathers. While every parent recalled a meaningful encounter when they were able to cry alongside a caring friend, they appreciated the ability to choose when and with whom such shared moments occurred. By receiving emails, texts, or voicemail messages, parents could respond on their timetable, when they were ready and wanted to. If you're wondering what is best to say, short messages conveying the following essentials were expressed by parents to be the most welcome means of reaching out:

> "I am praying for you."
>
> "I want to respect your privacy but I also want you to know that we are walking this journey with you."
>
> "I can't wait to meet (name of the new baby). Please let me know when you are up for a visitor."

One mother shared that her husband would not ask for emotional support or show appreciation when men from their church small group checked on him. But when the emails and texts began to drop off, she noticed her husband's emotional state began to deteriorate. Privately, this mother contacted the other wives in their couples small group. She shared how much their spouse's support had meant to her husband, even when he hadn't responded. Gratefully, word made it back to the men of the group, and the brief texts, emails, and voicemail messages to her husband resumed. In her emotional interview with me, this mother expressed her gratitude for the men in their church small group who left short messages in the early weeks after their child's Down syndrome diagnosis.

Each parent processes information and emotions associated with their child's diagnosis at their own pace and time. And if a medical condition is not part of their newborn's diagnosis, some parents may not feel the need for support until later, when behaviors associated with the child's diagnosis begin to surface or milestones have been missed. So, keep in mind that a mother or father who seems to ignore your words of support or offer to help in the early days after a new diagnosis may later welcome and even need to hear those same sentiments. You may need to remove the awkwardness for the family by initiating an interaction and reminding the parent(s) that your desire to help still stands, especially on significant anniversaries. One idea is to set a calendar reminder to reach out again to the family on the child's birthday or even the anniversary date of the child's diagnosis. Many parents reflect on the diagnosis date with great emotion. Pray for God to prompt you with the ideas to most effectively support a specific family. And be aware that mailing a simple card or sending a brief email or text is often appreciated—even at a later date.

Relational Etiquette Question #4
T/F—When talking with parents who have recently received a special needs diagnosis for their child, help them to see the positives in the situation.
Answer: False

Talk Less, Listen More

Keep in mind that, in the initial stages after parents have learned their child has a disability, nothing you can say will lessen the pain and grief they may be experiencing. In fact, well-meaning expressions can be perceived as an effort to diminish the feeling of loss. Even well-intentioned quotations of Bible verses such as Romans 8:28—"And we know that in all things God works for the good of those who love him, who have been called according to his purpose."—can feel like a trite attempt to place a Band-Aid on the pain. When the diagnosis is still fresh, do not pressure parents to focus on the positive about the situation. Doing so suggests that the parents aren't allowed to grieve. When they shared privately with me, many parents spoke of their appreciation for friends who created a safe environment where they could express authentic feelings of sadness. Remember that mourning is both biblical and healing. Doing anything that might repress a person's need to grieve is both uncaring and unhealthy.

"Mourn with those who mourn." (Romans 12:15)

"There is a time for everything and a season for every activity under the heavens . . . a time to weep . . . a time to mourn." (Ecclesiastes 3:1, 4)

One parent interviewed on this subject shared:

"Three years after the birth of our daughter with Down syndrome, I can tell you that if God—today—offered to take away her diagnosis, I think I would turn Him down. We love our child exactly how she was created. But in the days following her birth and diagnosis, I didn't want to hear passé clichés like, 'special needs children are a blessing.' I was grieving because this sweet girl would not live the life every parent envisions for their child. As I visualized her future, I saw a child who would attend far more doctor visits and therapy sessions than play dates and birthday parties over the course of her lifetime. Now, I am in a great place. I see Emma Kate* as a blessing, and when we do go to therapy, she loves it. But as we adjusted to Emma Kate's diagnosis, I needed friends to meet me in my grief and allow me to be authentic in my own feelings."

*Name changed for privacy.

Relational Etiquette Question #5
T/F—Be prepared to address theological questions with a family in the early stages of processing a special needs diagnosis.
Answer: False

In the midst of a special needs diagnosis, the gift of presence is more appreciated than an attempt to address all the big theological questions. While some parents may ponder hard questions related to their child's disability aloud, they may not be ready yet to explore the biblical answers, or lack thereof. Even if the family is wrestling through theological issues related to their child's diagnosis, it is less important that the church leader be prepared to provide answers right now, than it is they enter into the pain with the family. Instead of searching for the right theological solutions in the moment, ask for God's guidance on what to say and what not to say. The single greatest desire from families was for their church friends to join them in their grief. Receiving validation for their feelings of loss was more important to parents than receiving an explanation of that loss. It usually takes weeks if not months (and sometimes years) before one or both parents are ready to process God's purpose for their suffering.

> **Even if the family is wrestling through theological issues related to their child's diagnosis, it is less important that the church leader be prepared to provide answers right now, than it is they enter into the pain with the family.**

One mother shared that the most meaningful act of love and support that she received was the night her church small group asked to visit in her family's home. Shortly after the baby was born, the small group leader informed the rest of the members (with permission) that the new parents were nervously awaiting test results to determine whether the baby had a life-altering diagnosis. The small group immediately responded with one singular purpose: to listen.

> "These six other couples provided us with a meal and just fellowshipped with us. They took turns holding our baby and loving on him the way they would any other child. Everyone listened without judgment. They allowed my husband and me to openly share our fears. Then each group member took a turn praying for us. We knew that each person in the circle that night was walking in our pain. Many group members wept as they prayed. The words in their prayers reflected that they were imagining themselves in our place and they understood us."

The power of presence and simply listening to others share their story and pain can never be overestimated. In every interview, mothers shared well-meaning, but often stinging, comments just shortly after receiving their child's diagnosis. Parents repeatedly talked about the typical sentiments expressed by Christian friends that, although well intentioned at the time, came across as painfully dismissive. The following phrases should not be said to parents, and provide no comfort:

> **Receiving validation for their feelings of loss was more important to parents than receiving an explanation of that loss.**

"God doesn't give us more than we can handle."

"Special needs children are a blessing."

"God chose your family for this child."

"Everything happens for a reason."

Any statement that begins with "At least . . ."

Relational Etiquette Question #6
T/F—Ask to hold the baby when visiting the family just after the baby's birth and diagnosis.
Answer: True

Parents do appreciate friends and church representatives who offer greetings of "Congratulations!" to celebrate the arrival of God's newest creation. Although interviewed parents grieved the loss of what they imagine their child's life might be like, they always expressed a desire for their child to be celebrated. Interviewed families recounted moments when they silently cringed while sensing that visitors were afraid to touch their baby. And while there were medical issues preventing the infant from being passed around in some of these cases, families still loved being asked permission to hold their newborn.

One mother recounted the fond memory of a children's ministry leader who came to her hospital room shortly after her child's birth. This church leader was perhaps the first or only visitor who conveyed a desire to hold the baby. And while the mother had to say "no" due to the doctors' guidance, she loved the fact that her church friend wanted to touch her baby. Many interviewed mothers appreciated the people who visited who weren't afraid of their child and wanted the chance to "love on" their baby. Families yearned to hear positive comments, such as noting the beautiful features of their child.

 Relational Etiquette Question #7
T/F—If you know of another family with a similar situation, arrange for them to connect with the new parents.
Answer: False

One of the most common and well-intentioned mistakes interviewees described was when friends tried to connect new parents to another family who had a child with a similar diagnosis. Mothers shared that often the situations were not similar, caused unnecessary anxiety, and that in the beginning, the interactions were draining rather than helpful. In the early days after the diagnosis, parents have little emotional capacity to process new information, let alone another family's story. In addition, receiving stories and pictures of a child further along the special needs journey may be more discouraging than inspiring. This is especially true for parents still wrestling through the acceptance stage of their child's diagnosis.

Every interviewed mother expressed a desire to *eventually* connect with other parents who could understand their own situation. But, they wanted to seek out those relationships in their own time, when they were ready. Several mothers recounted the emotional energy required to listen to and relive another family's story, especially when they were already physically exhausted with a newborn and the emotional work of processing the realities of their child's special needs. Parents often grew weary of explaining why another child's outcome was different and potentially irrelevant to their own child's prognosis. There were exceptions to this in a few cases, where a child had an extremely rare condition. In these cases, the parents were sometimes desperate to find out more about their child's diagnosis and needs, which could include appropriate medical care. But in those situations, the family actively pursued asking for assistance in connecting with others. If in doubt, ask the family first whether they want to be connected with others walking a similar journey.

Relational Etiquette Question #8
T/F—Research and recommend support groups and treatment plans for the parents.
Answer: False, but with an exception

When reflecting on the relationships that did endure, parents spoke of friends and family members who gave them space and time to accept their child's diagnosis. Interviewees were quick to distance themselves from people who pushed them toward treatment plans or support groups before they were ready. If the mother felt a friend's pressure to pursue a certain type of therapy or join a parent support group, the natural inclination was to pull away from the relationship. While well intentioned, unrequested suggestions and opinions felt insulting.

> In the early days after the diagnosis, parents have little emotional capacity to process new information, let alone another family's story.

The exception was when the mother perceived a close friend's willingness to research treatment plans for the purpose of empowering her and sparing her some tiring legwork. In those cases, the assistance was appreciated; the mother could focus instead on meeting the needs of her child. But in general, mothers preferred retaining control over making choices for their child and for themselves.

One parent shared that she distanced herself from family members who had been on the Internet developing opinions. At the same time, there was one friend she had who quietly investigated doctors and therapy options right after the baby was born. This friend would make time-consuming phone calls to clinics and then to the family's insurance provider, figuring out what options were available and a good match for the child's needs. Every few days the friend would pass along the filtered information she had gathered. The mother said this friend wasn't trying to influence the family's decisions but instead helped the family to wade through the tedious and time-consuming deluge of information. The reality was that the mother herself didn't have the time or the emotional bandwidth to do the research immediately following the baby's birth. In this case, the friend respected the mother's aptitude and prerogative for making the best choices.

Prepare for the Child inside the Church

As the parents emerge from a period of initial shock and grief, they appreciate a church staff that initiates talking about how they will partner with the parents so that the child is an active part of the church. Interviewed mothers spoke fondly of children's ministers who approached them after the baby's birth or diagnosis to assure them of appropriate accommodations. One mother recounted a meeting she was invited to when her baby was several weeks old.

> "The children's pastor arranged for me to meet with my infant's anticipated caregivers. I shared the unique medical issues that could pop up during childcare and how we handled them. Looking back, I think this meeting was probably more for my comfort and assurance than it was for educating the children's ministry workers. But by having the meeting, when we returned to church, I was able to hand off my baby without hesitation and enter the worship center free of anxiety."

Parents feel a greater connection to their faith community when they observe visible ways the church makes accommodations for their child. Anticipating the individual needs of the child speaks volumes to the still-fragile family. And in cases where the parents do approach the church staff with requests or concerns, a warm response is crucial. While not every request can be fulfilled, the manner in which the concerns are received greatly influences how the family perceives

The manor in which the accommodation requests are received greatly influences how the family perceives the church's support.

the church's support. Even a small change can send a big message of love and acceptance to a hurting family. Consider the following ways to ease the entrance of a child with special needs into the church setting:

- Create reserved special needs parking spaces near a convenient church entrance.

- Enlist a host team to help a family get from the parking lot to the nursery.

- Train church greeters to respond to a first-time guest who may be impacted by disability. (See chapter 7 and appendix 7.3 for an outline and description of a training event for church hosts and Sunday morning greeters.)

- Pad the preschool or children's ministry with additional volunteers or "buddies."

- Recruit a volunteer nurse to serve at the preschool or nursery check-in desk for the duration of childcare.

- Keep allergy-free and other appropriate products on hand (e.g., latex-free gloves, gluten-free snacks, etc.).

Please keep in mind that there is no "once-size-fits-all" prescription for conveying support to every family walking through a special needs diagnosis. Giving and communicating love requires the person offering those things to know and appreciate the person receiving them. The same principles are true when it comes to conveying love to the family processing their new baby's special needs diagnosis. The best way to connect with such a family is to recognize what's unique about their life story. Your support is felt when they see your desire to join them in bearing their burdens.

These situations always require prayer and the guidance of the Holy Spirit. No book can offer those things. My hope with this chapter, and those that follow, is that you would gain a better understanding of experiences common to the family walking the special needs journey. And perhaps you would have a better idea how to pray when petitioning God to provide you wisdom in connecting with a specific parent of a child with special needs.

2. Loving the Family through the Diagnosis: Neurological-Related Diagnosis in Preschool or Elementary School Years

I n the first chapter, we covered how to support and minister to the family who receives an at-birth or early special needs diagnosis, including key insight from parents in interviews.

In this chapter, we explore the second type of special needs diagnosis, which also results in a unique family experience. The guidance shared in this chapter expands beyond the original interviews I conducted several years ago, and is the result of a longer period of research and writing on this topic.

Over the past four years, I have lost count of the number of mothers of children with autism, and other complex diagnoses and learning disabilities, who have given me the benefit of their valuable time and insight. The guidance offered in this chapter is the result of these wonderful parents as well as special needs ministry leaders who have shaped my understanding for how churches can better support these families.

Please note that every person and every parent processes a special needs diagnosis differently. If you know someone affected by a similar diagnosis, please pray for discernment as you read this chapter. Some of the following information may be helpful, while other guidance could be less relevant to a particular individual or family.

For a variety of reasons, the grief process and appreciated support differ for the family processing the diagnosis of a developmental disorder. For parents navigating a path forward for their child with autism spectrum disorder, pervasive developmental disorder, Asperger syndrome, and other similar conditions, it is important to understand their journey to diagnosis. While the diagnosis may be fresh, there is rarely shock when a name is finally assigned to the child's long-suspected neurological challenges. The time period between the first hint of a potential problem and the official diagnosis can be at least several months if not years. More often than not, the family has gone through multiple medical providers in order to find professionals that can properly recognize, diagnose, and treat the disorder(s) affecting their child.

Grief and Hope

By the time there's an official diagnosis, a mother may feel simultaneous emotions of grief and relief. Interviews revealed that during the diagnosis journey, at least one person in the mother's circle questioned or even criticized her child-rearing abilities. Perhaps she discovered a parenting book left in her mailbox by an anonymous source. Or possibly her mother-in-law reminded her of the value of and biblical instruction for "a good old-fashioned spanking." As much as a parent hates the idea of something being "wrong" with their child, the diagnosis may actually affirm a mother's intuition and parenting skills. Indeed, upon diagnosis she discovers beyond a shadow of a doubt that her instincts were right. Her child's behavioral differences served as an indicator of his health (physical or mental), and ***not*** as a reflection on her parenting skills.

> **During the diagnosis journey, at least one person in the mother's circle questioned or even criticized her child-reading abilities.**

Once a formal diagnosis is in hand, parents can focus their efforts on seeking the right assistance from professionals, schools, and advocates. Before the diagnosis, parents have likely pursued multiple avenues to try and find help for their child, wondering if it was a processing disorder, neurological disorder, anxiety, or a developmental delay as the root problem. With a diagnosis, some guesswork may be removed and the child may now qualify for publicly funded programs or therapies. The school system may also be able to provide intervention services to help the child and the rest of the family.

For parents, the prolonged journey to diagnosis can be filled with uncertainty. Often emotional and physical support has been needed but not necessarily provided along the way, before answers or therapy become available. Parents have processed many emotions privately long before they have voiced a desire for assistance from relatives and friends, let alone their church family.

> **If the parent is hopeful, don't judge them for being in denial. And if they are grieving, don't urge them to look on the bright side.**

For a number of reasons, some parents do not reveal their child's diagnosis openly. But if and when word makes it out that a family has received a diagnosis such as autism, mothers generally appreciate *private* inquiry. Furthermore, in interviews it was revealed that mothers and fathers often process the diagnosis at a different pace. In addition, parents do not always share the diagnosis immediately with the child affected or their siblings. As a result, friends should refrain from broaching the subject in the presence of others. Before approaching the parent privately, pray for discernment and be sensitive to how receptive they may or may not be to talking about this. You might start a conversation with questions:

> "I know the journey to an autism diagnosis involves many emotions. Where are you emotionally today? How can I support you?"

> "Do you feel relief having new information or does this feel overwhelming? How can I support you?"

> "How can I pray for you today? How can I pray for your child today?"

Listen: Always meet the parent wherever they are on the journey, remembering Romans 12:15, "Rejoice with those who rejoice; mourn with those who mourn." Allow the parent to be authentic, recognizing that they are likely processing a myriad of emotions. If the parent is hopeful, don't judge them for being in denial. And if they are grieving, don't urge them to look on the bright side. Concentrate more on focused listening and being fully present.

Pray Aloud: Consider praying aloud for the parent (ask them beforehand if they would like for you to do so), allowing them to know you are envisioning yourself in their shoes. Petition God for His gifts of wisdom and endurance as the parent must now assume a more involved and physically demanding role as their child's advocate. Before praying, be sure to listen for God's discernment. Don't pray aloud if your intuition (the Holy Spirit!) doesn't lead you in that direction. And please tread lightly when offering prayers requesting healing or complete healing. Later in this chapter, we will discuss the sensitive topic of prayer and the request for healing in special needs circles.

Difference, Not Disability: While grief is a natural part of any special needs parent's journey, it may be processed somewhat differently for the family affected by a diagnosis with a wide range of outcomes, such as autism. Every child with or without a disability is unique. And no special-needs diagnosis affects any two children the same way. However, the range of possible outcomes varies dramatically with an autism diagnosis when compared to other disorders and disabilities. In fact, using the term "difference" rather than "disability" is often more appropriate when describing how autism manifests itself in some individuals.

Sudden bursts of unexplainable improvement are not uncommon on the developmental path for a child with autism. So, a four-, five-, or six-year-old that isn't meeting developmental milestones may surprise everyone months or years down the line, when the child suddenly (and correctly) emulates instruction they failed to achieve at an earlier time. Along the same lines, not every individual diagnosed on the autism spectrum has an intellectual disability. If we performed an in-depth study of some of society's greatest contributors, I think we would find many of them had signs of learning differences or weaknesses with social skills associated with autism. College professor and best-selling

> Mothers are more likely to be real when friends give them permission to both hurt and hope.

author Temple Grandin is a widely known example of a person with autism who has achieved notable success and much admiration.

So, should a mother grieve the life she envisioned for her child? Or should she buckle herself in for a bumpy ride—remaining hopeful and doing everything humanly possible to help her child reach his or her full potential? Interviews with mothers revealed the dichotomy and dilemma of grief versus hope. If a mother places an emphasis on hope, friends may accuse her of being in denial. Conversely, if she grieves publicly or openly conveys her concerns, she may shape others' view of her child. In fear of creating a self-fulfilling prophecy for her child's future, parents often remain tight-lipped about the child's diagnosis. In some interviews, mothers shared that they intentionally avoid conversations revealing their daily realities out of fear that their friends would only see the child's disability, rather than their ability.

Mothers are more likely to be real when friends give them permission to both hurt and hope. Respect a parent's assessment of their child's aptitude and abilities. And recognize moments when you can be a genuine cheerleader to the mother and her child. Consider asking the mother questions like:

> "In your experience or observation, how is parenting a child with autism different than parenting a child without autism? How is it similar?"

> "Reflecting on your child's personal development, where do you see him or her growing and excelling?"

The Fear of Exclusion

Few things feel as threatening to a mother as does something that jeopardizes others' love for and acceptance of her child. The autism diagnosis is a big label that justifiably feeds a mother's greatest fears for her son or daughter.

- Will he sit alone at the lunch table every day at school?

- Will she ever be invited to a birthday party?

- Will he be the easy target of a neighborhood or school bully?

- Will teachers resent her for the extra work her IEP (Individualized Education Plan) creates for them?

Unfortunately, exclusion of the individual with special needs can even occur within the family. Perhaps another family member has not fully embraced the diagnosis for their son, niece, or grandchild. If that relative has reconciled themselves to their child's realities, they may struggle to view the child as having the same value and worth as the siblings without a disability. As a result, it is not uncommon for parents (and especially mothers) to lack full family support as they seek accommodation and help for their child.

> **When family ministry teams understand this fear of exclusion, they can better understanding why so many parents choose not to reveal their child's diagnosis to the church.**

When family ministry teams understand this fear of exclusion, they can better understand why so many parents choose not to reveal their child's diagnosis to the church. While some parents worry that staff leaders may refuse care for their child, often the fear of peer rejection is the bigger reason they choose not to share. In fact, some parents turn down the opportunity for the church to provide a one-on-one buddy if they perceive that this will impact invitations for shared play dates, children's birthday parties, or parent social events. This situation may be especially true inside churches where social cliques have emerged among the children or the adults.

Ultimately, helping families to feel valued and included can be achieved through intentional leadership on the part of the family ministry team. By identifying and engaging key influencers in the ministries (respected volunteers and parents), ownership can be created to promote special needs acceptance and inclusion. This may require addressing the issue of fear directly with these ministry partners and encouraging them to connect one-on-one with families affected by special needs. For churches that have parent support teams for their children's ministry or student ministry, consider placing a family that has a child with special needs on that team. Find ways to facilitate interaction and acceptance between all families, including those with special needs.

Disclosing a Diagnosis: Before I move on in this chapter, I want to address the issue of disclosing a child's diagnosis. When parents don't empower a children's ministry team with information to successfully care for their child, everyone loses. As a longtime children's ministry volunteer, I believe parents do owe some information to those who care for their child. Parents have a moral obligation to share knowledge about their child when that information could significantly benefit or protect the actual child, caregivers, other students, and the church staff. While it may require a measure of vulnerability to candidly share about a child's challenges or coping strategies, it's the right thing to do. Concealing information about a child's health or behavioral history may jeopardize the ministry. Thankfully, many churches are going to great lengths to facilitate success for children with behaviors that could otherwise compromise safety (see chapter 8 for more on this topic).

> Parents have a moral obligation to share knowledge about their child when that information could significantly benefit or protect the actual child, caregivers, other students, and the church staff.

Create an Open Atmosphere that Invites Disclosure

When parents observe a church culture of acceptance, they are more likely to disclose their child's diagnosis. And some parents may choose not to reveal the child's exact diagnosis but will candidly share about a child's unique needs (without sharing a specific label) and how the church can tailor an accommodation plan accordingly. Knowing the exact diagnosis isn't important. Understanding how the church can appropriately accommodate the child is important. As families gain a true feeling of acceptance, others inside the church are likely to begin revealing their child's differences or diagnoses as well. A church staff and family-ministry team may consider the following ways of visibly showing they accept and love individuals with differences:

- Wear official autism awareness jewelry, lapel pins, and lanyard ribbons. These can be ordered through www.SupportStore.com or www.AutismLink.com.

- Celebrate Autism Awareness Month each April. On the ministry website or monthly newsletter, provide tips for relating to a child with autism. With permission, feature an affected child's story from the church.

- Plug in students with differences or disability into visible places inside the church. During the large group experience, invite a student with special needs to say a memorized line as part of a skit. Ask a student with a disability to carry the flag during the Vacation Bible School assembly.

- Invite parents of children with unique needs to serve on the children's ministry advisory team.

- Arrange for the mothers' church group (e.g., MOPS) or Bible study to host a professional to speak on developmental milestones. Ask the speaker to address potential learning delays and autism education.

- Through in-person interviews or media presentations, spotlight families with special needs in the worship center, on the church website, and in other communication pieces.

- Partner with the church's care ministry team to meet the physical and spiritual needs of a family of a child with special needs.

Remain Focused on the Mission; Avoid Controversial Topics

With the explosive growth in autism diagnoses (1 in 68 children),[1] related news stories are common in the mainstream media. Often a headline will surface tied to a purported cause of or cure for the neurological disorder. Several years ago the autism vaccine controversy was debated in the media almost daily. These news stories run because they generate controversy and reader interest.

As a church, we need to be very careful about developing and expressing opinions on these topics. Even autism-related diets and therapy plans can spark considerable disagreement among good people. One mother may talk about the development improvements she's seen after using the Greenspan Floortime Approach with her child. Another parent or professional will share of the success of ABA (Applied Behavioral Analysis) techniques.

> **As ministry leaders and volunteers, it's our job to care most about a family's connection inside our church (and ultimately with Jesus Christ).**

Occasionally, professionals and parents will develop such strong opinions on these topics that discussion can turn inflammatory when disagreement emerges. The fact that there is not a consensus among professionals or parents for autism treatment plans is one of several reasons that I believe the church setting is *not* the ideal venue for therapy or intervention. We discuss the role of therapy and the church in greater detail in chapter 4.

As ministry leaders and volunteers, it's our job to care most about a family's connection inside our church, and ultimately with Jesus Christ. When any member of the family ministry team, including a child's volunteer caregiver, advocates a position related to autism causes, cures, treatments, or even diets, the church's influence is potentially diluted. Good people feel strongly on both sides of these issues. And their views and experiences are unique and real to them. As church leaders, our opinions on these topics aren't necessary to effectively love and support families who have children with disabilities. Encourage ministry team members and volunteers to remember the calling of the church: to enable families to develop a growing relationship with Jesus Christ.

If a parent wants to talk about their experience and it relates to an aforementioned (and potentially controversial) topic—wonderful. It is important for families to be able to share their experiences openly, and to be received without judgment. Church leaders and volunteers can listen and interact during such conversations. The important thing to remember is that the staff person or volunteer's opinion isn't necessary in order to remain engaged. And if the church person expresses their own views, they may inadvertently offend this family or another family participating in the ministry. The priority for the parent is simply a safe environment where they can talk about their daily life. Without taking sides on the controversial issues related to special needs, we can engage in a relationship with the families, many of whom are deeply hurting.

Similarly, a church staff member should carefully screen outside organizations seeking partnerships through the church's special needs ministry. Churches with large special needs ministries are often contacted by third parties offering assistance or looking to solicit a service or product inside the ministry. Sometimes these organizations and individuals can provide value to the participating families. Other times the third parties' involvement or association may be a distraction to the true mission of the church. It is never a mistake to ask questions and get references before partnering with a vendor and even a parachurch ministry.

> **Without taking sides on the controversial issues related to special needs, we can engage in a relationship with the families, many of whom are deeply hurting.**

The Subject of Healing

The subject of healing and special needs is extremely sensitive among many families impacted by disability. I want to address this subject briefly, without delving too deeply into theology. Admittedly, I'm not seminary trained nor have I researched extensively on the subject of divinity and disability. However, I do believe in God's healing power and that He chooses to exercise His power on this side of heaven. My purpose here is to explain the sensitivity toward the topic of healing among parents of children with special needs. In order to have influence in the life of a family dealing with a child's disability, it is important to understand how the topic of healing may be perceived inside the disability community, and especially in autism circles.

The cause for autism and how the diagnosis manifests itself in any given individual is largely a mystery. A child with a diagnosis, who for a long period of time has shown no progress in a certain area of development, may suddenly (and in dramatic fashion) demonstrate mastery of a related skill. For example, a student who has spoken only two or three audible words may unexpectedly offer a whole paragraph of big words. In January 2013, the

National Institutes of Health released a study showing that some children accurately diagnosed with autism were capable of making such improvement that they would go on to lose that diagnosis.[2] Another unexpected attribute sometimes associated with an ASD diagnosis is the ability to memorize and recite a long script (e.g., a movie) or detailed facts that a child might normally find challenging if not impossible. These savant skills are in fact more common in the autism population.[3]

> To the secular world, without great care, dramatic and public claims of miracles and healing can portray Christians as not understanding the very nature and characteristics of autism.

I share these examples because it can come across as suspect and disingenuous when, amidst great fanfare, claims are made of God's miraculous healing after such an improvement or feat. We know that every good thing comes from God, so I'm comfortable praising God for a child's progress, breakthrough, or virtuoso abilities. But to the secular world, without great care, dramatic and public claims of miracles and healing can portray Christians as not understanding the very nature and characteristics of autism.

The topic of healing may be controversial for additional reasons. It is important that I'm not misinterpreted on this topic. Because of personal circumstances in my own life, I have sought the assistance of some serious prayer warriors. Together, we petitioned God to work inside my own difficult situation. I believe in the power of prayer and the importance of asking God for healing in our lives. In no way do I want the ideas expressed here to diminish the Bible's instruction to pray and my belief in God's power to do some pretty big things.

The point is to caution church leaders of the damage and disillusionment that can result when families perceive an imbalanced focus on healing inside their faith community. For those parents who do not experience complete or even partial healing for their child, a church's emphasis on healing may cause existing feelings of failure to mushroom. Parents may question why prayers for their child were unsuccessful and then blame themselves (consciously or subconsciously) for their child's suffering. In fact, God may be working in and through their circumstances, and we can't know completely how God is working through any situation during our earthly lifetime. But if the topic of healing is overemphasized, the family of an individual with special needs may miss the opportunity to be loved and accepted for exactly who they are and where they are in life. Again, the church's role is to provide a safe, nonjudgmental environment that enables families to experience the love of Jesus Christ.

Actions Speak Louder than Words

Countless mothers have given up careers and life passions in order to advocate full-time for their child. Even more impressive, many of these women refuse to be victims in order to make the most of life, for themselves, their child with special needs, and the rest of their family. Not coincidentally, this same group appreciates "can-do" life-helpers who are solution driven. Moms of children with special needs largely value action over sympathy. And this is especially true when these parents engage the church staff. Interviews have revealed tremendous frustration and even anger for instances when a church staff member said all the right things in terms of understanding the family's plight, but ignored a need for action. If a request for accommodation is not legitimately discussed and a solution at least attempted, extreme frustration may emerge. One parent interviewed shared the following illustration of this point:

> "At the time of Ashley's* Pervasive Developmental Disorder** diagnosis I was serving as the leader of our church's Moms-n-More group. It had come to my attention that Ashley (age three) was becoming a challenge in the nursery during our weekly Moms-n-More meetings. The single-room setting included two caregivers and fifteen children ranging from infant to pre-kindergarten age. Ashley's behavior was predictably disruptive when the infants started crying or the noise of children reached a point that the sensory stimulation was overwhelming. I felt that if a worker could take Ashley for a brief walk during these periods or if the children could be divided into two rooms, so that the crying babies were separated from the older children, then Ashley's frustration and disruptive behavior would disappear.

I finally decided to approach the church's children's minister and reveal Ashley's diagnosis. I was very emotionally fragile at the time. I tearfully shared our story and began a dialogue for how we could create a successful environment for all the children in care during our weekly mom's meeting. The staff member listened empathetically and said all the right things. I left the meeting thinking she wanted to help.

Several weeks passed without follow-up or any evidence of attempts to change the nursery setting. I never heard from the children's minister again. Ultimately, another mother in the group pressured me to remove my child from childcare during Moms-n-More. In humiliation, I resigned my position of leadership inside the church moms' group. Since that experience, we haven't returned to church and I find myself struggling with resentment and embarrassment."

Name changed for privacy.

**Pervasive Developmental Disorder is a diagnosis often associated with high-functioning forms of autism spectrum disorder.*

This doesn't have to be the outcome. The most appreciated interactions between the church and parents involve a visible effort to collect information for the purpose of devising a plan forward. Parents frequently shared of setbacks in their experience inside the children's ministry. But generally speaking, when reasonable efforts were being made toward accommodating their child and the overall direction was positive, they were very forgiving and patient amidst missteps along the way. If the parents felt they had a healthy line of communication with the children's ministry team and the church was following up in a timely manner, they tended to reflect on the setbacks less negatively. Parents were more likely to continue their involvement in the church if they perceived the children's ministry leadership was working proactively to appropriately accommodate their child.

Embrace the Parents and Recognize the Fears

Whenever a family approaches a member of the family ministry team (or any caregiver) with the news of their child's diagnosis, it is crucial that they are received with gentleness and acceptance. One interviewed mother shared about her exchange with her children's minister shortly after receiving her son's autism diagnosis.

"Our son was struggling to potty train past the acceptable age for most preschoolers. Due to church policy and toileting arrangements, I decided to reveal his diagnosis in order to explain his challenges. I didn't know our church children's minister very well and I dreaded the needed conversation. Tearfully, I can now recount the meaningful way she embraced me and eased my anxiety. She listened to my story and cried along with me. Then she asked if the church could assign my son a class helper. She covered all the logistics for his care. After we worked through his accommodation, she then looked at me and said, 'How can I pray for you?' Before we parted, she requested permission to share of my son's diagnosis to a handful of other mothers on my same journey. Now I look back and see that my healing and personal path forward largely began in my meeting with the children's minister."

In several instances, I have observed a children's minister facilitate the introduction and appropriate pairing of a child with special needs with a caring peer. Many heartwarming stories have emerged where typically developing peers have been paired with a child with any number of special needs diagnoses. Very often, relationships and friendships are developed that extend beyond Sunday morning, creating lasting bonds between the families.

A Practical Guide to Including Children

A Practical Guide to Including Children

I honestly don't know how many church leaders I've talked with about special needs inclusion. Since 2008, I've been researching and writing on the topic of special needs and family ministry. When I sat down to write this section of the book—off the top of my head—I quickly recalled more than fifty church leaders and a dozen professionals who had significantly invested in my understanding of this subject matter. These were not people who contacted me with a question or need; these were people who answered my call, my email, or found themselves in a conversation where they were educating me. Through phone interviews, in-person meetings, and sometimes crazy-long email exchanges, they allowed me to extract years of experience from them and, God bless their souls, some talked to me until they were plumb wore out. A handful of these people have gifted me with so many hours of advice over the last several years that, frankly, I owe their spouses a mention in the acknowledgments. I can picture more than a few heads nodding affirmatively as I type these words.

The remaining chapters of this book portray a single viewpoint: mine. But the content is essentially a student's reflection on and compilation of what she has learned thus far from a large number of teachers. I have been mindful of presenting the material in this book in a way that makes each one of my "teachers" proud. However, not every opinion and idea in this book will be agreed upon by all who have influenced me. And not every assertion will be universally applicable to all readers and their church culture. If each reader gains one new idea that makes them a better friend or a better ministry leader to a family of a child with special needs, then the book has achieved its objective. This book isn't the Bible, so take what's useful and leave the rest.

Reflecting on several years of research, a general summary of my findings related to churches and inclusion of individuals (particularly children) with special needs is shared in the following section. This insight is an estimation and, at times, is opinion-based, unless otherwise noted. Candidly, I don't have scientific research to prove some of the assertions. The following nine generalizations are the result of the aforementioned interviews as well as the daily emails and calls I receive from my blog readers (TheInclusiveChurch. com) and other church leaders.

1. Special needs issues are affecting churches of every size. Congregations with a regular attendance from eighty to eight thousand are both impacted, as children with neurological and physical disabilities seek inclusion. Small churches and newly launched church plants are making incredible efforts to accommodate a single child or several children with special needs. Small churches with limited resource pools (fewer volunteers, restrictive facilities, smaller curriculum budgets) seem to have some of the most challenging situations, where a child or family is significantly impacted by disability and their successful inclusion requires a multi-step accommodation plan.

2. Churches identifying themselves as "seeker friendly" are more likely to have a special needs ministry. The larger the "seeker friendly" church, the greater the odds of having a formal special needs ministry. A high number of megachurches have a special needs ministry or are in the process of developing one.[1] Churches that have a special needs ministry or a coordinated plan for inclusion do not always disclose this fact on their church website.

3. Developing an inclusion plan for a single child can require an investment of time. Basic accommodation may require facility and logistical changes, caregiver coordination, and curriculum modifications. Many churches have a designated staff member on the children's ministry team who oversees the ministry while the day-to-day coordinator running the ministry is a volunteer. The rapidly developing trend is for larger churches to hire a paid staff leader to direct the special needs ministry under the umbrella of family ministry.

4. Many paid special needs ministry leaders have a college degree related to special education or pediatric therapy. A high number of special needs ministry champions (especially those who serve in a volunteer capacity) have someone in their immediate family who has been impacted by disability. Few special needs ministry leaders worked on staff at a church prior to this serving in their role. Understanding the culture and politics of the church frequently adds to the learning curve for this ministry leader.

5. Churches with developed special needs ministries receive a high number of inquiries from other churches. It is not uncommon for a special needs leader to spend 25 percent or more of their time providing free consultation to other churches looking to start a special needs ministry. Neighboring congregations are more likely to work together and help the other succeed when it comes to special needs ministries. It benefits everyone for more than one church in an area to provide specialized accommodation for children and teens with special needs.

6. Two U.S. states seem to have more churches with special needs ministries: Texas and California. Due to the high concentration of megachurches with sophisticated children's ministries, the Dallas and Houston areas have a number of comprehensive special needs ministries. California also appears to have a notable number of churches with special needs ministries, especially in areas of the state that have been reported as "autism clusters."[2]

7. Autism is the most significant factor driving the increased need for special needs ministries. The number of ASD diagnoses has risen dramatically in recent years.[3] In addition, the higher survival rates associated with premature births[4] has contributed to the growing need for special accommodation as disabilities associated with the preterm birth remain the same.[5] Another factor is the increase in international adoptions of children with special health needs.[6] For more statistics relating to these factors, see chapter 3.

8. Many children's ministry teams have at some point sought guidance related to accommodating a child without an identified disability but who exhibited signs of a neurological disorder. In a number of those cases, the child's safety or the safety of others was a concern.

9. As a student with special needs progresses in age, successful inclusion inside the church becomes more complex.

While not every observation proves true with every church, it is from these assumptions and generalities that the content for this book has been developed.

3. Special Needs Statistics, Terms, Laws, and Trends

At some point, every family ministry team realizes there's a child or teen that needs extra help in order to be successful in the church environment. Perhaps the parents have approached the church with a request for special accommodation. Or maybe a ministry volunteer noticed a child with behaviors or needs not being met. Thankfully, many churches have responded warmly to an attending child's unique challenges by providing a buddy or staffing a special needs classroom. While a reactive approach to disability accommodation has been the norm, it's time for all of us to get prepared. Kids with diagnosed and undiagnosed learning differences are attending (or attempting to attend) all of our ministry environments. Without adequate planning, it's very likely that families with special needs will feel unnecessarily frustrated and stop participating. Our volunteers can also be affected if we don't think about our responses and options in advance. When a church proactively prepares for special needs inclusion, we make a more seamless integration of the person with special needs more likely, and everyone wins.

19 percent of Americans of all ages are classified as a person with a disability

The Statistics

According to a 2010 U.S. Census study, 56.7 million Americans, or about one in five U.S. residents, have a disability. And about half of those with a disability report it as being severe. Between 2005 and 2010, both the percentage and number of Americans with a severe disability rose as did the number and percentage of Americans needing assistance.[1] Statistics also tell us that among children ages 3 to 17, 14 percent have a developmental disability.[2] Consider the increase in the incidence of autism. Between 1997 and 2008, the prevalence of autism diagnoses increased 289.5 percent.[3] And by 2010, 1 in 68 children was identified with an autism spectrum disorder. The incidence rate among boys is actually as high as 1 in 42.[4] Some professionals argue that these statistics are still too conservative, only taking into account children who have been formally diagnosed with an ASD (autism spectrum disorder). A respected South Korean study identified as many as 1 in 38 children as exhibiting characteristics associated with autism.[5] With these statistics in mind, can any ministry ignore the need to prepare for participants with learning differences and disabilities?

- 1 in every 700 babies is born with Down syndrome. Between 1979 and 2003 this number increased by 30 percent.[6]

- 1 in every 68 children have been identified with an autism spectrum disorder.[7]

- 11 percent of children ages 3 to 17 have been identified with ADHD.[8]

- 8 percent of children ages 3 to 17 have been identified with a learning disability.[9]

- 14 percent of children ages 13 to 17 have been identified with a developmental disability.[10]

- 17 percent of Americans are estimated to experience a communication disorder at some point in their life (1/6 Americans).[11]

- 19 percent of Americans of all ages are classified as a person with a disability (more than half of these report the disability to be severe).[12]

- 25 percent of 13- to 18-year-olds are identified with anxiety disorders. 6 percent are considered to be severe.[13]

Common Terms and Phrases

Person-first Language: The most appreciated way to refer to a person with special needs is by placing focus on the person first, before naming the disability. It is more sensitive, acceptable, and politically correct to say: "a child with autism" or "a student with Down syndrome" than to say "an autistic child" or "a Down's kid."

Intellectual Disability (ID): Intellectual disability is a general term for what has previously been described as mental retardation. ID is a lifelong condition characterized by significant impairment of cognitive and adaptive development and is a general symptom of neurologic dysfunction. This terminology is preferred over the previously used term "mental retardation," or MR. While the latter term is still used by some clinicians and in legal policies, it is generally found to be offensive when used in everyday language.[14]

> It's never acceptable to use the phrase "retarded" when referring to persons with intellectual disability.

Intervention: Intervention refers to the planned strategies or educational programs designed to produce behavior changes, academic progress, or health improvements for an individual or group of individuals.[15] In everyday terms, intervention may refer to speech therapy,

occupational therapy, physical therapy, academic instruction, medical treatment, and/or behavior treatment plans.

Typical Peer: A typical peer refers to a typically developing child or
student. When the term is used in conjunction with a reference to a child
with special needs, it is assumed that the typical peer is of the same age as
the child with special needs.

Typical Setting: A typical setting or class refers to the environment(s)
where typically developing students are learning and/or participating in
planned activities.

Self-Contained Special-Needs Setting: A self-contained environment
is designed with appropriate activities and adapted curricula to accommodate individuals with additional needs while also meeting their social and
emotional needs. When associated with church programming, this designated environment may be an optional or preferred setting for some individuals with special needs, unique sensory needs, and/or additional safety
supports to prevent elopement. "Elopement" is discussed in greater detail
in chapter 8.

Inclusion or Mainstreaming: Inside the public school system, the
terms *inclusion, full inclusion,* or *mainstreaming* refers to the concept of educating a child with special needs in the same class as their typically developing peers. Often this typical setting that includes the child with special
needs will involve adapted curricula, additional aids, and personally dedicated staff, all to help the child with special needs excel.

In the context of the church, inclusion is a broad term that can mean
many things related to including a person with special needs inside the life
of the church. Ideally, church inclusion is achieved when both of the following occur simultaneously:

1. The family impacted by special needs feels welcome and part of
    their faith community;

2. The church develops an accommodation plan for the child with
    special needs that benefits the child and works within the capa-
    bilities and available resources of the church (accommodation plans
    are further discussed in chapter 5).

Reverse Mainstreaming: Placing one or more typically developing children in a designated special needs environment to learn alongside and interact among children with special needs.

Partial Inclusion: Partial inclusion means that a child with special needs is included in the typical setting for part but not all of a school day or program environment. This approach is commonly carried over into the church setting. For example, a child may participate in activities alongside their typical peers for a certain length of time as long it is appropriate. If the child communicates a desire to leave the environment or indicates the participation in the typical is no longer beneficial (e.g., overstimulation, sensory needs, etc.), the child may then change to an alternate environment such as the special needs class.

Individualized Education Plan (IEP): An IEP is a formal education plan required by law for public school students receiving services for qualifying special needs. This plan is developed on an individual basis by a team of interested parties (parents, school faculty, intervention providers). An IEP creates goals for the student and the means for their achievement within the public school system. Education and intervention providers involved in a child's IEP process have responsibilities associated with the IEP, which is a legally binding document with the school. (Individualized Education Plans are not required of churches.) IEP meetings occur at least annually to discuss the progress of a student and set goals for the following year.[16]

Significant Support Needs (SSN): Students with significant support needs are highly diverse learners with extensive needs in the areas of cognition and/or learning, communication, movement and social/emotional abilities. The individual may also have concurrent health, sensory, physical and/or behavioral disabilities and often requires a wide variety of approaches and supports as well as individualized supports across major life activities in home, school, and community.[17]

1 in 68 children is identified with
an autism spectrum disorder

Least Restrictive Environment (LRE): By law, public schools are required to provide a free appropriate education (FAPE) in the least restrictive environment that is appropriate to the individual student's needs. LRE means that a student who has a disability should have the opportunity to be educated with non-disabled peers to the greatest extent appropriate inside public schools. Students with a disability should have access to the general education curricula or any other public school program that non-disabled peers would be able to access. And through tax-funded public schools, the student should be provided with supplementary aids and services necessary to achieve educational goals. Because the individual needs among students with disabilities varies so broadly, there is no single definition of LRE. In many cases, it requires teams of professionals to work with the parents and the public school in order to create and agree on the "appropriate" and "least restrictive" educational environment.

The Impact of Autism

Just as every typical child is unique, every child with special needs is unique. No two children with the same diagnosis will exhibit identical gifts or challenges. This is especially true for children who have an autism spectrum disorder (ASD). There is a reason autism is referred to as a *spectrum* disorder. The closest synonym for the word *spectrum* is the word *range*. For the child with autism, there is a vast range of possible outcomes. One child may have limited cognitive, verbal, and physical abilities. Another child may be incredibly intelligent, highly verbal, and possess the physical strength of an ox. And for many kids with the diagnosis, they may have a combination of any of the above attributes. It is important to note that **46 percent of individuals with autism do not have an intellectual disability.**[18] This is why using the descriptor "differences" rather than "disability" may be more accurate when speaking of the special needs of a higher functioning child on the spectrum.

> Just as every typical child is unique, every child with special needs is unique.

An ASD diagnosis is also not necessarily a predictor of an individual's life path, as many diagnosed persons go on to earn college degrees, pursue successful careers, and have fulfilling social lives. So often, a student with autism will have more in common with their typical peers than with other kids sharing the same diagnosis. And this scenario impacts the way we map out special needs inclusion in the church setting. Largely attributable to the nature of autism, we've seen less emphasis on special needs classrooms and a growing use of one-on-one helpers or "buddies" as part of a church's special needs accommodation plan. Establishing buddy rotations have become increasingly important to the success of a church's special needs ministry. And the most progressive churches are going further by designing experiential large group and small group settings for all kids that offer visual, auditory, sensory, and kinesthetic learning opportunities. By engaging multiple senses, these experiences increase the odds of connecting with a wide range of participant learning preferences and abilities.

About one in five U. S. residents have a disability.

The Impact of the Law

Since 1975, Congress has enacted several significant pieces of legislation shaping the special education environment and other publicly funded programs assisting persons with disabilities. Based on the ***Individuals with Disabilities Education Act (IDEA)*** and ***No Child Left Behind Act***, the current trend in public education has moved away from self-contained special education classrooms and toward inclusion. Wording such as "least restrictive environment" is common guidance provided by the laws for the schools' placement of children with disabilities. How each state and each local school system interprets and applies the law is often different and complicated.

Parents' expectations for their child's placement and experience inside the church are often shaped by the practices inside the public school system. For this reason, it is helpful to have at least basic knowledge of how schools accommodate and integrate kids with special needs into the school setting. In many cases, best practices from the school system do translate well to the church setting. And in other situations, accommodation plans and strategies that are successful in the school system may not be practical or possible for the church. **Because churches are not publicly funded organizations, their capabilities will be limited compared to the supports, space, and staffing that a school is required to provide.** Churches are not held to the laws IDEA sets forth for public agencies and schools.

The *Americans with Disabilities Act (ADA)* was enacted in 1990 and has had a significant impact on virtually every business and organization in America. ADA guarantees equal opportunity for individuals with disabilities in public accommodation, transportation, and employment. Restaurants, theaters, doctors' offices, parks, private schools, and day care centers, to name just a few, must make reasonable changes in policies, practices, and procedures to avoid discrimination. **These entities may also be required to provide special aids or services to individuals with disabilities so that they may participate in or receive benefits from the services/products provided.** These same entities are required to alter their existing facilities or build new ones to ensure accessibility.[19]

While churches are currently exempt from *some* aspects of ADA compliance,[20] the law still impacts our houses of worship and faith communities. As a general rule, it is easier (and frankly more honorable) for a church to worry less about any exemptions from ADA and more about how they can comply when making their facilities physically accessible. Many states have additional accessibility and anti-discrimination regulation that apply to religious organizations anyway.[21] Fortunately, the standards set forth in ADA have provided sweeping changes in building design that have carried over into the construction of new commercial buildings, including churches. Thanks to ADA, America is a more physically accessible place to live.

Note: Childcare centers run by religious entities (e.g., church has direct control over the program and in turn, the facility is not being rented/leased to a childcare provider), are exempt from Title III of the Americans with Disabilities Act. However, many aspects of Title III are reasonable and good guidelines for a church. The "Disability Rights" Section of the Civil Rights Division of the Justice

Department provides excellent guidance in a 1997 document: "Commonly Asked Questions about Child Care Centers and The Americans with Disabilities Act": http://www.ada.gov/childqanda.htm I recommend that churches become familiar with the related guidance and do their best to adhere to similar standards as followed by secular childcare providers.

The Impact of Societal Trends and Universal Design

The laws explained previously in this chapter have run parallel with developing views in society regarding accessibility. Accessibility means more than adding a ramp between the sidewalk and the front door of a building. It includes the ease with which a product, service, or environment can be utilized across diverse "human populations, their abilities and their needs."[22] A popular term that's being heard more and more is ***universal design*** which seeks to make virtually everything "more accessible, safe, and convenient for everyone."[23] While these ideas originated with a desire to better enable participation by individuals with disabilities, the philosophy extends even further by encouraging design that takes differing cultures into account.

> It's the church's responsibility to thoughtfully, intentionally, and respectfully engage everyone—because God loves them all.

A similar, new trend in the development of modern products and services is the notion that they should be ready for use by as many people as possible and without the need for adaption.[24] We see this most prominently in the architectural industry where "handicap accessible" products and configurations (e.g., door handles, faucets, etc.) that were once special orders or custom are now standard. The philosophy also carries over into the field of education where thought leaders wisely argue that teaching methodologies and curricula used in the typical classroom should more naturally encompass a wide range of learning styles and abilities.

All of these trends impact the church, but one thing in particular stands out: A growing number of churches are taking note of these things and making adjustments in order to remain relevant and engage all of their communities. They are working hard to establish thriving special needs ministries and the communities respond. This isn't just a matter of staying relevant. We must ask ourselves, "If visitors come to our church, will they feel that we are accepting and accessible to people who are different than us?" Repeatedly in Scripture, we see stories of Jesus engaging individuals who were unlike Him, many of whom the society of His day did not value or respect.

We as the church do not want to lag behind society today, in terms of welcoming people of differing cultures, races, and abilities. Practically, this plays out many ways—thinking about others and our differences when we design ministry space, produce videos for the worship center, select praise songs, and develop curriculum. It's the church's responsibility to thoughtfully, intentionally, and respectfully engage everyone—because God loves them all. That's the gospel being lived out for all to see and experience.

4. Establishing a Mission for the Special Needs Ministry

If you want to build a successful special needs ministry, determine your goals. When you as a church define the goals and parameters of the special needs ministry, success becomes a more achievable outcome. Without a communicated and clear plan, disappointment and even dissention may emerge. This is often because parents and other church members with an interest in this growing ministry naturally start to formulate a more personal vision for the ministry around their own life circumstances and needs. This is to be expected, because each of these parents have had unique and different experiences shaping their hopes and expectations. And because so many parents have traveled a long, emotional path with their child, it's not uncommon for their opinions, once voiced, to be emotional and charged with passion.

However, parents and other interested people often *don't* know the specifics of the church culture, overall goals of church leadership, and resource limitations. So, if you don't state the special needs goals and ministry parameters from the beginning, feelings can get hurt easily, and relationships may be damaged, even though everyone has the best intentions. To avoid misunderstandings, let's talk about how we determine the goals of ministry. We'll start at the most important place—making it all about Jesus.

Free the Ministry to Focus on Jesus

I attend a church with one mission: **To "lead people into a growing relationship with Jesus Christ."** So, that's the filter with which I write this chapter. I believe the goal of every church ministry is to point people to Jesus. If your church holds similar views, then it is easier to narrow and clarify the focus of the special needs ministry. I would argue that everyone wins when the ministry is freed to focus on Jesus. Let me explain. While it is optimal for a child to learn to read and write, those skills aren't required in order to develop a personal relationship with Jesus Christ. In fact, I *don't* expect God to ask any of the following questions to people standing at the gates of heaven:

During your time on earth,

> *Did you master your ABCs?*
>
> *Did you produce legible handwriting?*
>
> *Did you manipulate scissors, pencils, and other utensils correctly?*
>
> *Did you look people in the eye when speaking to them?*
>
> *Did you learn good conversation skills?*

God cares about our personal development, as it relates to our intent to worship, honor, and glorify our Creator. And we can praise and glorify God without necessarily answering "Yes" to any of the above questions. If a kid isn't particularly strong at reading or writing, no one in the ministry environment needs to push him to improve. Of course, there will be times when students who are capable of reading and writing will resist such an activity. And that's when a caring leader who knows the child well can use his or her judgment in the situation. But generally speaking, if a participant with special needs has an aversion to reading or the inability to write, the volunteers should assist the child or look for an alternative way to engage the child in the ministry environment.

It can be a similar situation for a student who struggles with social or interpersonal skills. A child or teen with special needs may show significant discomfort, sometimes through their behavior, in a particular ministry setting or in certain types of peer interactions. While we all need to be nudged outside of our comfort zone occasionally, it is important for church leaders (and parents!) to recognize that a nudge can quickly turn into an anxiety-inducing "push" for many kids with special needs. If Jesus is the focus of the special needs ministry, then the church is less concerned with nudging a student toward better social skills and instead more concerned with placing the student in an environment where they feel comfortable and can experience success. A Jesus-focused ministry gives greater weight to connection over correction, recognizing that change and spiritual growth occur in the context of meaningful relationships. The student with special needs is more likely to develop a personal relationship with Jesus if no one is hung up on the deficit in interpersonal skills and instead everyone cares more about providing a positive, anxiety-free church experience. We all know that it is difficult to process new information, wonder aloud with questions, and enjoy ourselves in a setting where we feel anxious or nervous. And we more naturally experience Jesus' love in environments where we feel comfortable and unconditionally accepted.

Ultimately, the student, the volunteer, and the family benefits from a narrowed, Jesus-focused special needs ministry, and here's why:

The child can enjoy church. No one enjoys working on things that are hard for him or her. And that's no different for the child with special needs. So often, these kids already have spent long hours during the week in educational and therapeutic settings being pushed to catch up to their typical peers. And that may be wise and necessary for the child. But let Sundays be for rest and worship. In fact, that's biblical!

> "Six days you shall labor and do all your work, but the seventh day is a Sabbath to the LORD your God. On it you shall not do any work, neither you, nor your son or daughter." (Exodus 20:9–10)

When the special needs volunteer or buddy is encouraged to take a more laid-back approach, they have the opportunity to foster an authentic relationship with the child. The educational and therapeutic settings are all about achievement. But that isn't what a relationship with Jesus Christ is about. He loves us exactly as we are and He wants a relationship with us regardless of our performance. We can't earn His love or His grace. He gives it freely, without holding anything back. And it is so important that we model that kind of relationship for participants with special needs. Very often, children and teens with an intellectual disability or learning difference require a concrete experience in order to grasp an abstract concept. To many kids with special needs, their church relationships will correlate with their understanding of Jesus' love for them. So, when we can remove objectives for academic and social achievement from the church setting, we give kids the chance to have fun and experience a Christlike love.

The special needs ministry becomes a place where "serving is a pleasure." Most special needs ministry volunteers are good-hearted lay servants without professional training. They want to love the kids they're serving, and they want those same kids to love them back. If an expressed or unspoken pressure is felt by volunteers to further a child's academic, behavioral, or social goals, volunteers are likely to feel inadequate for serving in the special needs area. And if a ministry culture emerges that implies there is a "right way" of teaching, feelings of frustration and even failure are sure to follow among the volunteers. Because there are so many viewpoints on special education, behavior modification, and therapy, it is difficult if not impossible to build a ministry team that is united on these various approaches. If a strong personality within the ministry begins advocating a particular approach to education or behavior management, a church leader may need to establish boundaries and remind them of the church's calling. A ministry is much more likely to retain its volunteers and the families it serves (who often have diverse views themselves) when a hard and fast devotion to certain education and therapy philosophies are kept out of the church environment. (For a greater explanation of the differing philosophies and controversial subjects, see chapter 2.)

> The educational and therapeutic settings are all about achievement. But that isn't what a relationship with Jesus Christ is about. He loves us exactly as we are and He wants a relationship with us regardless of our performance.

Personally, I believe the success of a volunteer is almost as important as the success of a child. I write from the perspective of a volunteer because that's what I am and always have been in my own church. If the expectations for the special needs volunteers evolve past what the average church member can provide, then the days of the special needs ministry may be limited. To my best recollection, every church I've ever interviewed relies on unpaid servants to propel the special needs ministry. (Some churches do utilize paid staff for respite and special needs summer experiences, but that type of ministry is not what is being discussed here.) So, if a church can reduce the responsibilities of the volunteers down to the mission-critical objectives of the ministry (ensuring safety and pointing to Jesus), then the volunteers are more likely to experience success and keep coming back.

One church leader who directs her church's special needs ministry candidly shared the following with me:

> "A crucial part of my role is setting everyone up for success. Managing the expectations for what our ministry can do and not do is part of my job description. So, when a new student enters our program or when I am working through an inclusion strategy for a particular student, I'm always mindful of keeping the child's accommodation plan achievable for the volunteers. When action steps are agreed upon that fail to consider the limitations and personal lives of our ministry volunteers, odds are we will lose a ministry helper or eventually a family when unmet expectations begin to surface."

While thinking through the importance of creating a positive environment for volunteers, the slogan of a prominent grocery store chain comes to mind. In Atlanta where I live, I shop regularly at a particular chain that claims to be a place "where shopping is a pleasure." And their ads are right! I buy my groceries at their store because they have anticipated my needs and removed some of the less desirable aspects of grocery shopping before I even arrive. I'll admit, this chain doesn't always have the lowest prices. But I go there because I enjoy walking down the well-designed aisles. I am usually able to get in and out of their stores in minimal time and the employees *always* treat me with respect. As church leaders, part of our job is to create ministry environments where serving is a pleasure.

As church leaders, part of our job is to create ministry environments where serving is a pleasure.

And one way we can do that is by tempering the expectations placed on volunteers and simplifying their responsibilities. Eliminating any secondary agendas is always a good thing.

The parents can enjoy their own small group or worship experience. We know that, if a child enjoys church, he's less likely to pose behavior challenges while in church care. (We'll address behavior challenges ahead in chapter 8.) And any time we can create a ministry atmosphere conducive to positive behavior, we've spared the parents a headache, at the very least, and a serious barrier to attendance at the most. By simplifying the goals for the child's church experience, the child is more likely to thrive in church. And, Mom and Dad can peacefully bid adieu when they arrive at the child check-in area. Of all the goals and outcomes for a special needs ministry, there is one that is the most important: To enable parents of kids with special needs to attend their own worship and Bible study. After all, any child (with or without special needs), has the greatest opportunity to experience the love of Christ when they are raised by parents with a mature faith of their own. Hopefully, your church's family ministry team is already focused on equipping *all* parents. And so, as special needs ministry leaders, our most crucial objective is to facilitate successful accommodation for the child with special needs so that Mom and Dad can receive their own spiritual nourishment.

Create Guiding Ministry Documents

By its very nature, special needs accommodation is more individualized than the typical children's ministry. And as we talked about in the introduction to this chapter, each family of a child with special needs has hopes and expectations for their child's church experience that stem from their unique life experience. As a result, any time a ministry leader has to address what the church's special needs ministry can do, can't do, will do, and won't do, the conversations are poised to be sensitive and possibly even emotionally charged.

One of the best things a church can do to reduce the number of delicate (if not damaging) conversations is to create and publicly post guiding documents for the ministry. Consider publishing the mission statement inside any marketing materials about the ministry, the volunteer and parent handbook(s), as well as the church website. You might even display the ministry's mission statement on a wall in a public place, such as core values that are seen posted at a place of business. Communicating to people the purpose of the ministry will help them frame their expectations of the ministry and their subsequent requests. Generally speaking, people are less likely to take in-print guidelines personally.

Establish a ministry mission statement. In one or two sentences, create a statement that gives the overarching goal of the ministry. While this declaration should be broad, it should also be specific enough to serve as the filter for the ministry. In other words, when any addition or change to programming is considered (either for the whole ministry or for a specific individual), it should be held up and considered in light of the ministry mission statement. This helps to keep the big picture in mind. Proposals that involve partnerships with outside organizations, individual parent requests for accommodation, curriculum changes, new or additional hours of programming, and any general ministry expansions should be analyzed with questions like: "Does this opportunity/change help us to achieve our ministry objective?" or "Does this opportunity/change detract from our mission?"

The special needs ministry mission statement should support the overall mission statement of the church. If your church doesn't have a published mission statement, then ask the senior pastor to provide some guidance. Every church is unique. The location, culture, demographics, available space, financial resources, personalities of the leaders, and core theology will shape the mission of any given church. As a result, church mission statements vary. A special needs ministry statement is unlikely to survive the test of time (or help a church) if it doesn't align with the broader church objectives.

Every church should tailor their statement to their own culture and capabilities. I recently read the mission statement of one church's special needs ministry that was narrower than the example we provide in the sample mission statement at the end of this chapter. This church's special needs ministry's stated purpose was to "break down barriers that keep children with disabilities, grades K–6, and their families from being able to participate in the community of the church." Some readers may be disappointed that this church's ministry and mission statement only cover one age range of church participants. But I say kudos to the children's pastor who got the ball rolling and did what she could inside her own area of responsibility and authority. This particular church's ministry document went on to spell out in some detail goals for accommodation that were specific to children's ministry. As that church expands its special needs inclusion to more age groups, I can see where they may have different documents with slightly different goals for each ministry area (student, adult, etc.).

Identify Beneficiaries of the Ministry

A church doesn't necessarily need to spell out who the ministry serves or how a student is "signed up" for its services. However, I have provided wording in my sample mission statement (at the back of this chapter) that may help churches in need of a backdoor way to utilize the services of the ministry. And what I mean by "backdoor" is that sometimes it is a church leader or volunteer, not the parent, who requests the services of the ministry on behalf of a particular student. Without the help of the ministry, the success and/or safety of a particular individual's church participation may be in jeopardy.

Let me explain. Frequently I receive a phone call or email from a church along these lines:

> We have a child whose parents have never mentioned anything about their son/daughter having any special needs. He/she participates in our typical ministry environments. However, the child's small group leaders have observed recurring behaviors that are causing a problem and these behaviors are often associated with a special needs' diagnosis. Our attempts to broach the subject with the parents have proven unsuccessful. Can we place the child in a special needs ministry without the cooperation or consent of the child's parents?

A slightly different variation of the story involves an older student, often a teen, struggling with appropriate emotional responses for his or her age. While the behavior doesn't necessarily threaten anyone, it is disruptive. The church leader contacting me may also be concerned that the student is embarrassing themselves among their peers. Whether the situation involves a child or a teen, by the time the church has reached out to me the leaders and volunteers have already invested quite a bit of energy and time trying to figure out how to solve the problem.

In both of these scenarios the most difficult aspect of the situation is not the child's behavior. The real issue is the fact that the church doesn't feel they have an open relationship with or support from the parents. In churches that care about special needs inclusion I have found that the single biggest determinant for a child's success is the strength of the relationship between the church and the child's parents. When church leaders and parents are in general agreement regarding a child's abilities and needs, problems tend to get solved with greater speed and ingenuity. But when parents view their child's special needs as nonexistent or insignificant, it creates extra work (and stress!) for everyone serving that child. This is the reason that it is sometimes easier for churches to successfully include children with complex needs that are obvious than it is for churches to successfully include high-functioning children whose disabilities are less obvious. When parents dismiss a child's legitimate need for even occasional assistance it makes it really hard for the child and the volunteers serving them to experience success.

In the scenarios I've just described the church may already have a good idea how to solve the behavior problem with the child. They have likely tried a couple of things before they called me. And they may know that the child does much better when he or she has the regular assistance of a special needs-trained buddy or that the problem behavior disappears when he or she is chilling out in the church sensory room.

> When church leaders and parents are in general agreement regarding a child's abilities and needs, problems tend to get solved with greater speed and ingenuity.

The question churches often have in these situations is primarily around how to help the child without the parents' partnership. It requires an abundance of prayer and discernment to initiate and utilize the services of the special needs ministry without the involvement of the child's parents. However, there are times when this is the *only* way a particular ministry participant can enjoy a safe and successful church experience. And this is why I have added a statement in the sample mission statement that makes a provision for a church leader to request the services of the special needs ministry. We'll talk more about concerning behaviors and safety in chapter 8.

Clarify What the Ministry Can and *Cannot* Do

A mission document can also be the place where the church formally expresses the limitations of the special needs ministry. A clarifying statement such as the one we show in the sample document may remove ambiguity regarding the goals of the ministry. Everyone wins when the parents, volunteers, and church leadership start the ministry on the same page, with everyone understanding the purpose and capabilities of the ministry.

By having a statement in writing addressing the services the ministry does not provide, odds are higher that parent expectations are kept in check. This is important because a common source of conflict between parents and a ministry's leadership is the fact that the church staff or volunteers failed to meet parent expectations. And unfortunately parents don't always realize they are carrying expectations until they experience disappointment. When the church spells out up front and in writing what it cannot do or will not do, that disappointment and other unnecessary hurt feelings are more likely avoided.

Medical Assistance

In our sample mission statement, we address the issues of medical assistance. For the purpose of our example, we say that the church won't provide medical intervention. We'll talk about this more in chapter 7 when we address ministry policies. However, a number of well-run special needs ministries are actually prepared to dispense medicines and offer medical assistance. Many churches include children who are medically fragile. How a church handles the issue of medical assistance is up to each church and each ministry environment setting. During summer church experiences with longer hours, it is common for a church to contract a nurse for Vacation Bible School, day camps, or overnight retreats. It's wonderful when a church has the resources to provide a nurse to render treatment or dispense medications as needed. In those cases, I would advise a church to contract a third-party agency that can employ, train, and carry the liability insurance on the skilled provider. It is also imperative that the church ask for input from their insurance provider when developing ministry practices pertaining to medical care.

Exceptions

I have written this chapter assuming we are talking almost exclusively about accommodating children with special needs in the context of *regular, weekend church programming*. And the vast majority of the ideas and recommendations I discuss throughout this book apply to other church environments, such as Vacation Bible School, Wednesday night programming, and so forth. However, I want to address an exception. I am familiar with several churches that offer optional classes or summer experiences to help kids with special needs further their social and academic goals, and I think these efforts and services are incredible! I know of two churches that have, at one point or another, put on a drama camp aimed to help kids with autism spectrum disorder. Another church offers social skills workshops on a recurring basis for interested parents and students. And I am aware that many churches with special needs ministries host seminars to help parents navigate the unique academic, financial, social, and health needs of their children with special needs. I'd love to be part of those ministries! These camps, workshops, tutorials, and events are great outreach for the community and they beautifully support families already inside the church who are impacted by special needs. With that being said, the purpose of this chapter is to outline the goals for the ministry as it relates to caring for and teaching the child with special needs while participating in regular church programming.

———

Sample Wording for Special Needs Ministry Mission Statement

The purpose of our church's special needs ministry is to facilitate inclusion inside the life of the church for the individual with additional needs and for their family. In support of our broader church mission, the ultimate goal of the special needs ministry is to lead individuals and families affected by unique needs into a growing relationship with Jesus Christ.

The objective(s) of the ministry are fulfilled through the ministry's efforts:

1. To create an accepting church environment for the family impacted by special needs or disability.
2. To develop an appropriate accommodation plan and/or supports for the individual with additional needs while working within the policies and resources of the church.

3. To equip leaders and volunteers in various ministries across the church to help them better include individuals and families affected by special needs.

The services of the special needs ministry may be requested by the individual themselves, the family of the individual, or the ministry leader(s) serving the individual.

For the purpose of the special needs ministry, the terms "additional needs," "special needs," and "disability" encompasses a broad range of unique needs, including but not limited to: learning differences, intellectual disability, neurological disorders, developmental delays, communication disorders, social skills deficits, physical disabilities, sensory needs, and medical conditions. A student experiencing a significant life-change may also benefit from the services of the special needs ministry for a period of time (e.g., placed with an assigned buddy or in an alternate learning environment). Understanding why a particular individual requires the services of the ministry is often unimportant. What is important is that the ministry is able to provide assistance in order to help individuals with special needs experience success in the church setting.

Our church's special needs ministry does *not* provide therapy, behavior modification programs, or medical intervention. To the best of our abilities, our ministry servants will strive to follow guidance from and utilize tools provided by parents. And, medical assistance will be provided in emergency situations.

5. Developing an Accommodation Plan for the Child with Special Needs

Many children's or student ministry teams have felt conflicted at some point in how to best accommodate a specific child with special needs—a student's temperament and learning preferences vary from one week to another; another individual who thrives in the small group setting reacts poorly to the bright lights and loud noises of the large group environment; or the team games and group dialogue of small groups pose a challenge to the same student who relishes time in theater-style large group. As if those variables weren't enough, often the gifts of a particular leader factor into the small group or class placement of the child as well. And last but not least, the desires of parents (often for greater socialization) frequently influence the student's inclusion plan.

Dr. Alyssa Barnes, who holds multiple degrees in the field of special education, helped me understand this. She explains: "In the public school system, the classroom placement of children with special needs is one of the most controversial issues. So, the church should not find it surprising when it too struggles to find the perfect accommodation plan for a child with a complicated set of needs." Barnes continues:

"In government-funded schools, placement decisions involve a team of opinions. The placement process sometimes requires mediation or even due process procedures to settle on a specific child's learning environment and education path." As a result, churches can expect that it may take time and perseverance before a student with special needs is successfully woven into the church setting.

Inclusion Models and Strategies

In 2010, I launched the blog theinclusivechurch.com to help churches better include children with special needs. I wanted to create a venue for my ongoing research and writing. Before the blog, I spent as much time working to find publications to publish my research and writing as I did producing the content. I also wanted to provide a central place to address questions that church leaders had begun posting as they came across my articles or heard me teach a workshop. I couldn't always answer the questions myself, but I often knew experienced ministry leaders who could.

Thanks to the suggestion of a friend and longtime ministry leader, I decided to launch a blog about all things related to special needs and children's ministry. It soon evolved into a place where seasoned special needs ministry leaders could be spotlighted and offer their own best practices. Through the experience of running the blog and its associated social media accounts, I've received a crash course in what topics stir debate the fastest among special needs professionals and parents. Frankly, it still surprises me at times to see the topics that create spirited, and occasionally less-than-pleasant, comments via social media or emails to me.

> There is no single way for a church to do special needs inclusion that will please everyone.

How a church defines and applies their intent to "include" children with special needs is one of those sensitive and often controversial topics among parents and professionals. After dozens of interviews, I have learned that there is no single way for a church to do special needs inclusion that will please everyone. And it is very important for the church leader, especially those unfamiliar with the world of special education, to come to terms with this reality. Some approaches will satisfy more people than others, and that can be important. But, as much as a church does their best to develop an accommodation plan suited to the individual needs of a specific child, someone somewhere will disprove the approach the church and the parents agree to. There are many differing philosophies in education circles as well as unique personal experiences of other parents, which naturally shape their views. Good people disagree on how a church should run virtually every ministry inside a church, and this is especially true for special needs ministry. Below, I provide guidance on developing accommodation plans and defining inclusion, knowing full well that not every reader will agree with my viewpoint. And that's okay! As I've said before, "This book isn't the Bible. Take what's useful and leave the rest."

> This book isn't the Bible, so take what's useful and leave the rest.

When developing each child's accommodation plan, it is more important to arrive at an agreement with that child's parents than it is to earn approval or appreciation from third parties who are outside the situation or outside the church.

There are three approaches to church accommodation and inclusion that we'll focus on in this chapter:

1. One-on-One Assistants (Buddies): The church provides a personal buddy to accompany and assist the child with special needs inside the typical ministry setting and among typical peers. For the remainder of the book we'll refer to this accommodation approach as the "buddy system."

The use of "buddies" is the most common strategy for church inclusion. Many kids with special needs can successfully participate in the typical ministry environment with the aid of a one-on-one helper. This assigned and trained volunteer may adapt an activity on the spot, remind the child of upcoming transitions, or provide familiarity and comfort to the participant with additional needs. Generally speaking, this is the preferred method of accommodation, partially because it closely mirrors the approach utilized by many public schools. And it works for many kids with special needs, especially those who are high functioning and may have more in common with their typical peers than with others who share their same diagnosis. Oftentimes, kids with special needs can adapt more easily than we realize and little is needed to yield success. I love the buddy system partially because it provides a concrete picture of the personal relationship Jesus desires with each of us and it reminds us of the relationship He modeled with

His disciples. It should be noted that children with special needs and their typically developing peers are generally already accustomed to this type of accommodation arrangement because it is what many experience inside their public school environments.

2. Self-Contained Special Needs Setting: The church staffs a room with a lower ratio of participants to volunteers than the typical ministry settings. This room might provide alternate activities that participants with special needs may enjoy such as puzzles and toys. The class may also offer a Bible lesson with enhanced visual aids and modified learning exercises adapted from typical children's ministry curriculum. This environment is designed to better engage participants with learning differences. Often, the atmosphere and pace of this class is more individualized than the typical children's ministry setting.

The churches that offer specially designed self-contained settings are generally able to accommodate a wider range of students, especially those with more complex needs. While the buddy approach is more popular and sometimes easier to implement, it may not be enough to ensure that every individual has a place they feel comfortable or can succeed inside the church. The self-contained environment very often has its own sense of community and a more relaxed culture. Nearly always I observe these environments to be unconditionally accepting of quirky mannerisms. And while the typical children's or teen ministry setting may need to become more accepting of socially awkward behaviors, it's virtually impossible for those places to ever match the laid-back, "nothing surprises us, no, not ever" culture I often experience in an environment especially designed for special needs. This culture can be so helpful for the individual who wants to remember but struggles to tone down the one or one hundred quirky behaviors. Instead of working so hard to act in a socially acceptable way, that student is freed to be who they are and to fully engage in the Bible lesson and relationships around them.

> The churches that offer specially designed self-contained settings are generally able to accommodate a wider range of students, especially those with more complex needs.

In addition and perhaps most important, the self-contained special needs environment may be the only place some individuals have the opportunity to learn about Jesus in a meaningful way. Because special needs designated settings are more likely to offer adapted Bible lessons with concrete illustrations, enhanced visual aids, and multi-sensory learning experiences, students with learning differences are more likely to connect with the truths being taught. Stay with me here, this point can't be missed! The self-contained special needs environment may be the one and only venue that facilitates the spiritual growth for some students because it's the only place that Jesus is shared in that individual's native language. We get this concept when we talk about offering worship services or Bible studies in different languages within our congregations. Now, we need to "get" and apply this concept when we are talking about individuals with disability or learning differences. Students with all kinds of challenges can learn and grow in their faith. We just need to provide them with worship services and Bible studies in their native language, so to speak. And what's crazy is that sometimes when a church gets it right and provides Bible stories and learning experiences in these students' "native language," somebody out there is beating the drum, criticizing them for not being fully inclusive. That criticism isn't always fair. Don't miss this: While full inclusion inside our churches is ideal, that goal is secondary to making the gospel fully accessible. When considering the proper placement of any student of any ability, the first concern should always be positioning that individual in the setting with the culture and the teaching methods that best facilitate meaningful spiritual growth for them.

> **The goal of full inclusion inside a church is secondary to making the gospel fully accessible.**

3. Hybrid Approach: A church sets up a buddy system while simultaneously providing a self-contained special needs setting. By offering both options, students may participate in the environment(s) best suited to their abilities and needs at a given time. Some students may actually participate in both settings (the typical ministry environment and the special needs class) in the same day. For other kids, their accommodation plan may vary from week to week, depending on many factors such as new medication regimen, the previous night's sleep, home-life changes, and so forth.

Inclusion Tip: Prepare a Buddy Clipboard

Offer a clipboard with the following communication pieces and aids for each buddy to access during their service on Sundays, Wednesday nights, or in VBS:

- **Participant-specific buddy communication sheet:** This communication piece provides an opportunity for the ministry leaders serving at check-in to communicate helpful information about the student directly with their buddy. The same sheet may be returned to ministry leaders with any notes from the buddy. These sheets should be saved and filed, as they may be helpful when identifying trends in a child's needs/behaviors and helpful when accommodation plans require an adjustment.

- **Weekly ministry communication sheet:** This communication piece may provide relevant information about the day's ministry environment, enabling the buddy to better meet the needs of the student. The same sheet may offer weekly updates and serve as a community-building tool inside the ministry.

- **Customized participant schedule:** Reviewing this schedule may provide a means of comfort to a particular student who struggles with transitions. Providing stickers to note the successful completion of the activities can make the schedule review interactive or reinforce positive behavior.

- **Additional learning page or activity sheet for the student to complete during a time they might otherwise become bored or disengaged:** If a buddy notices their participant becoming restless, they may pull out the activity sheet that matches the ability and interests of the student. Dot-to-dot pages, illustrated activities, and word finds that relate to the day's Bible lesson are great ways to engage a child and reinforce the Bible lesson.

In some ways, shopping at the local supermarket is a good teaching model to mirror how individuals interact in the real world. Real life is about working in the same space as persons with all levels of abilities. After all, there isn't a separate section or designated shopping day in any grocery store for individuals with disabilities. Supermarkets do not have special needs aisles that are separate from other aisles. In fact, shoppers of all abilities and differences move among each other in the supermarket, and it works well.

We help all children learn healthy ways of relating when we create environments that reflect real life. In contrast, we are doing the child with disability as well as the typically developing peer a disservice if we aren't looking for opportunities to facilitate their interaction. And as Christians, I would add that the church is naturally set up to adopt an inclusion mindset, because we follow Jesus and know He modeled love and value for all children.

Did you know that often the relationships that are fostered in the ministry setting carry over into everyday life and outside of church? Since researching for this book, I have learned of several friendships between an individual with special needs and a typically developing peer that started at church. Shared play dates and healthy interactions on the school playground are common outcomes (and great benefits!) when children with special needs are included in church environments among typically developing peers.

Inclusion Tip: Provide an In-Person Tour of Ministry Space Prior to Participation

Offer a tour of the ministry space on a quiet weekday. Simply having an opportunity to see the environment without the chaos can help remove the intimidation to a child who may otherwise experience anxiety or sensory overload. Consider inviting the student's buddy or perhaps even one typical peer to join the child on their church tour. Creating familiarity creates comfort and increases the likelihood of success.

Yet, even with support from buddies, some kids with special needs still need access to an alternate environment. One of the biggest reasons a student may need a one-on-one helper is so that they have the freedom to leave the typical church setting while being accompanied by their buddy. It is not uncommon for a participant with special needs to be successful in their typical setting for some, but perhaps not all, of the time in the church environment. A participant with special needs may benefit from time outside their typical small group or large group environments for any or all of the following reasons:

1. Sensory issues may arise during certain activities or in certain settings. Sensory processing problems are common attributes that accompany many diagnoses. In fact, many kids with no particular diagnosis still have sensory challenges. And, churches can be one of the most difficult places for kids with sensitivities or who have a tendency to get overstimulated. Behavior problems can actually be attributed to a child's reaction to an internal sensory discomfort. Common sensory challenges can include but are not limited to:

- Sensitivity to bright light

- Distress with loud noises or certain sounds

- Aversion to certain smells

- Uneasiness in high-energy settings

- Inability to self-regulate or calm down

- Certain sensory-seeking needs (e.g., physical activity, exertion, body compression, stimulation)

2. The child with special needs may not connect with the materials and activities in the typical setting. Sometimes the lesson plans do not play to a specific participant's skills or preferred learning style. And in these times, if a student is not engaging in the group's activities, he or she may become bored or even agitated. (Very often, behavior problems are a child's way of communicating frustration because they are unable to actively participate.) The option of leaving the typical ministry setting, taking a walk to a quieter area of the church, or retreating to a more individualized environment may be an important part of making the child's church experience positive. And to go a step further, the child can benefit even further from time in a small group setting where the Bible story and the learning experiences are tailored to their pace and ability.

3. A pattern of disruptive behaviors interrupts the ministry experience of others. Every kid has a bad day and deserves an occasional pass. But when those behaviors become frequent, predictable, and/or upsetting to the other ministry participants, appropriate accommodation might best occur in an alternate environment, outside the typical setting.

> Very often, behavior problems are a child's way of communicating frustration because they are unable to actively participate.

4. Additional safety supports are required for the successful accommodation of a particular child. One of the most critical responsibilities of the preschool ministry, the children's ministry, and the student ministry is to provide a safe environment for every participant, including the volunteers. When any of the following situations arises, a self-contained or secure environment may provide the appropriate accommodation for a specific student who has any of the following:

- Weakened immune system, requiring limited exposure to others

- Tendency to run away, bolt, or wander (called "elopement" in special needs circles)

- Behaviors that are inappropriate for a typically developing child of the same age (especially when those behaviors pose a direct threat to the health or safety of others)

5. The child needs a break. So often, a ministry participant can benefit from a few minutes or maybe even an entire day retreating from the busy, noisy, structured, or unstructured typical ministry setting. Occasionally, time rocking in a swing, or chilling on a beanbag chair, allows a child to relax and enables them to have a positive church experience. (I'd argue that such breaks are helpful for many kids participating in a children's ministry, not just those with identified special needs. We can be on the lookout for signs and help all children to be successful by providing an "out" occasionally.)

Inclusion Tip: Create a Virtual Tour of a Student's Church Experience

Through a video recording, walk a child through their entire church day from the arrival in the parking lot until they leave the campus. Send parents a link to the video to help their child visualize their trip through church hallways, the insides of the rooms they'll be participating in, and meeting some new faces who may be working with them during their time at church. This can be an important part of the transition plan for kids who will be promoting to a new grade or new ministry environment. Some kids may enjoy watching this video several times to prepare themselves for even the smallest of changes in their Sunday, Wednesday night, or VBS church experience.

Optimal Approach = Hybrid Approach: Ideally, a church provides buddies inside inclusive environments while *also* offering at least one self-contained classroom. (Many churches offer multiple special needs environments, some grouped according to participants' ages and others customized according to learning styles and preferences). However, offering multiple means for accommodating students with special needs is not possible for every church, especially smaller congregations. My goal for this book is to be an encouragement to all churches and church leaders. I hope this book will inspire every reader to go one step past their comfort zone when it comes to special needs inclusion.

For many churches, especially small faith communities, if they can start their ministry by offering either a buddy system *or* a special needs classroom, they are taking a huge step forward. A church's efforts to start one aspect of the special needs ministry should be applauded. Whenever I address this topic, I often hear from a few angry readers. Someone is always upset if a church launches only one type of environment and it isn't the type of setting that person believes to be politically correct or more effective. And then there are those that are angry that the church is failing to offer both types of environments, inclusion with buddies and a self-contained class. Let me take this opportunity to ask everyone who has an interest in this important topic to be cheerleaders to one another. So often, the angry voices don't know all the facts surrounding a church's decision or the unique needs of the families that church is designing their accommodation around. If a church doesn't have the volunteers, the space, and the resources to launch a ministry with every base covered, let's not chide them for getting it wrong. Let's cheer them on for taking a step in the right direction, for meeting the immediate needs in their midst, and for expanding their accommodation to any degree, and striving to do it well.

> "Finally brothers and sisters, rejoice! Strive for restoration, encourage one another, be of one mind, live in peace. And the God of love and peace be with you." (2 Corinthians 13:11)

Before we move on to the next idea, I would like to ask my fellow Christians to take a deep breath and pray before posting online comments and blog posts that are critical of churches. The loud negativity that occasionally surfaces on this topic deters some observing church leaders from taking a first step toward special needs inclusion. Justified and unjustified articles written about how one or many churches fail the individual or the family with special needs can create the perception that this population is difficult to please and has zero tolerance for well-intentioned trial and error. While there may be more to a story than "well-intentioned trial and error," sometimes it doesn't read that way to another church staff member who believes the best about their peers in similar positions at other churches. And the reality is that many ministry leaders fear failure and public rebuke. So when some church leaders see viral posts about churches getting it wrong, they fear they'll get it wrong too. They would rather avoid the situation altogether, ignoring any requests related to special needs because the last thing they want is to draw attention to their failed efforts. They don't want to become the thinly veiled inspiration for the next "10 ways your church can fail the child with special needs" or similarly titled blog post that makes all the rounds in Christian circles

> So often, the angry voices don't know all the facts surrounding a church's decision or the unique needs of the families that church is designing their accommodation around. If a church doesn't have the volunteers, the space, and the resources to launch a ministry with every base covered, let's not chide them for getting it wrong.

and on social media. While misperceptions and fears rooted in pride are not the responsibility of the person making an online comment or writing a public blog post, it is the Christian's responsibility to ask themselves if they know all the facts surrounding the situation and to ask God for discernment before hitting the "post" or "share" button. While these catchy titles and trending articles may generate attention for a cause we all care about, it may do more harm than help in the long run. If you want to influence people and motivate people to change, you've got to love them well. This truth applies to your relationship with your teenage son, your neighbor, your coworker . . . and your church leader.

Inclusion Tip: Graduated Inclusion

Be prepared for some behavior hiccups in the large group or other inclusion environments. Loud noises, bright lights, and the general chaos inherent to group settings may spur anxiety or sensory overload for a few kids. To acclimate these students, consider exposing them to the setting for a brief but increasing amount of time each week. For example, for the first week a buddy might walk a student to the back of the group setting, staying for under one minute and during a less rowdy time. The next week the goal may be to remain in the typical environment for two or three minutes. In time, perhaps the student stays through the duration of music or drama, and so on. You can expect to have a week when you backtrack, and that's perfectly okay! But by graduating the exposure, you are making progress. And at the end of a ministry year, you might see a child comfortably participating with their typical peers for the majority of the time. At checkout, be sure to celebrate improved participation to parents. Many families appreciate knowing that the church is working to help their child become comfortable in typical settings and among their typically developing peers.

Volunteer Placement: When accommodating children with special needs, volunteer placement is sometimes as important as child placement.

Occasionally, parents resist the idea of a buddy, in their effort to fully integrate their child among their typically developing peers and to provide a "normal church experience." In those instances when an appropriate accommodation plan and parents' wishes don't perfectly align, consider adding a trained volunteer to a specific student's small group. Discreetly position this additional helper with the understanding that they are tapped to assist the child with a disability or learning difference. This goal of a buddy should never be to isolate and separate, but to encourage and facilitate full participation to the best of the student's ability.

In cases where safety is a legitimate concern, placing an additional volunteer in an inclusive setting may not suffice. In some situations, a child's participation in the self-contained special needs environment may be the best or only option for a safe and successful church experience. It is advisable for churches to work with their insurance companies and provide a brief statement in their ministry handbooks reserving the right to remove a child from the typical ministry setting if their participation creates undue risk for themselves or any other ministry participant. We'll address this topic more specifically in chapter 8.

It is also worth noting that the strengths (or weaknesses) of a particular group leader may factor into the placement decisions for a specific child. I have heard of many situations where a child with complex needs is able to fully participate in a typical setting largely because of the gifts of a certain ministry leader. That volunteer teacher may naturally engage kids with learning differences or create a group culture that is more laid-back when it comes to interruptions from a child who lacks appropriate social skills. In fact, because of that teacher's approach, a buddy may not even be needed.

In contrast, there may be a volunteer leader who is wired a bit tighter and has less room for deviation when it comes to addressing unexpected behavior. A child who may otherwise be okay participating in a typical setting could potentially struggle under the leadership of such a teacher. And perhaps for those reasons, an accommodation plan is developed that involves less time or no time in the typical small group setting with such a teacher.

Some might argue that since the "problem" is the teacher, the group leader should be coached or removed. That may be true to a point. However, it is so important to note that volunteers lead virtually every church ministry team. There is no such thing as annual reviews or salary increases. These are unpaid volunteers. Churches nearly always need every single willing and qualified volunteer. As a result, the success of the ministry volunteers is often every bit as important as the success of the participating kids. And the skills of the ministry leaders do impact the accommodation plans that are developed for participants with special needs. So, I'd encourage you to work with what you've got—trying to find the best fit for everyone.

Inclusion Tip: Create "Exit Tickets"

Exit tickets serve as a personalized recap of what a child learned during a single experience in the ministry setting. A ticket might offer the child the opportunity to complete statements such as:

Today, I learned about _____.
Today, I prayed about _____.
My favorite thing from today was _____.

The group leader or the student's buddy may interview each participant, writing their answer or assisting them as they complete the statements themselves. (Note that this interaction time serves as great lesson reinforcement for the student!) For children who do not communicate verbally or through writing, the ticket may offer corresponding pictures for that day's subject matter or activities. The child can then circle or paste on graphic illustrations to serve as their answer. While a similar exercise is valuable for typically developing children, it can be especially cherished by parents of children with special needs who may appreciate evidence that their child is absorbing a basic Bible concept or participating in social interaction at church. The ticket may also serve as a great conversation starter for kids who struggle answering questions about what they did during their church participation.

Developing the Accommodation Plan for the Child with Special Needs

In order to craft a successful accommodation plan for a specific child, a church needs to understand that particular child's abilities, preferences, and unique needs. Creating and requiring the completion of a get-to-know-you type of intake document is the best way to determine how the special needs ministry can best serve the child and their family. This intake form and process is also crucial for the church in preparing for and managing any associated risks.

Intake Interview and Documentation

Creating written intake documents is paramount to the success and safety of everyone involved. In order to encourage parents to share more about their child's needs, it is ideal for the visitor and new member registration form(s) to have a single question prompting parents to reveal their child's unique needs. At the bottom of the same registration form that requires the child's name, date of birth, and parents' contact information, you might add the following statement and question:

Our church cares for the success and safety of each participant inside our ministry. Does your child have any allergies, medical conditions, learning differences, special needs, or other additional needs of which our ministry team should be aware? Circle one: YES / NO

If the parents circle "Yes," then the church associate assisting parents at the first-time check-in should ask about the nature of the child's needs. How to handle the "Yes" answer requires some judgment. If "Yes" is circled only because a child has an anaphylaxis reaction to peanuts, then the church can document and communicate this very important fact to relevant ministry leaders without going through the full, detailed, additional-needs intake process. In other cases, the full intake form may be needed, but the time to complete such a form may not be in the midst of a rushed and hectic Sunday morning.

It is important to make a quick assessment of the type of accommodation the child may require because sometimes more details are needed sooner than later. Most of the time, the church staff has to make an on-the-spot placement determination and then revisit the intake conversation in order to gather more facts and to make a long-term accommodation plan, after the Sunday morning dust has settled. When it comes to special needs inclusion and Vacation Bible School, the longer and more detailed questions usually need to be addressed immediately at check-in. VBS is different than Sunday morning accommodation because parents leave the church campus and the child is in the church's care for a longer period of time.

In a perfect world, the parents will have contacted the church ahead of time regarding their child's additional needs. To make this even more likely, I've seen several churches post links to their special needs intake forms through their special needs ministry page on their church website. One church posted the policy on their special needs ministry page, saying that special needs accommodation would only be provided after parents have completed an intake process. While this policy and posting is arguably extreme, I know the background behind the policy for that particular church, and there was wisdom in its development. As churches become more special needs friendly, we may actually see a rise in public requests for parents of children with special needs to contact the church prior to their first visit. It is important that the church be adequately staffed and prepared to provide safe care for every participant. And for this reason, it is sometimes necessary for a church to ask parents for one week's notice prior to providing specialized accommodation.

> **Intake forms are best completed as part of a relational conversation between the church and the child's parents.**

I believe intake forms are crucial to developing a child's accommodation plan inside the church. And for that reason, they are nearly always vital to the child's success. Intake forms should be completed in writing and kept on file at the church. However, I much prefer their completion as part of a relational and conversational process between a representative from the ministry and the family. Here's why:

1. Intake conversations allow the church to convey their intention to accept the child. Even though difficult subjects are often broached that require parents to be vulnerable about their child's needs, the ministry representative conducting the interview can provide assurance during the dialogue. The interviewer's voice tone and response can help the mother or father understand that the church is willing to work through challenges.

2. Intake conversations invite more candid disclosure. The church representative leading the intake interview can ask follow-up questions that may reveal crucial details that wouldn't have been divulged on a parent-completed form. Through the course of conversation, Mom may share a story that involves a success strategy from school that could apply to the church setting (and be an important element of the child's accommodation plan). So often, the dialogue between the church and the family uncovers valuable information about the child's needs or abilities that a form alone couldn't have captured. This information is helpful when making buddy assignments and determining which small group is the best fit for the student with special needs.

3. Intake conversations reveal other family needs. For many families of a child with special needs, developing a sense of belonging and connection inside a church is every bit as important as developing their child's accommodation plans. The ministry representative interviewing the parents has a unique opportunity to learn more about the needs of every member inside the family. The real "win" of an intake conversation happens when that church leader recognizes opportunities for connection and then makes relevant introductions to other church members and ministry leaders. Helping each member of the family, not just the child or teen with special needs, network inside the church and develop relationships may be the most important result of an intake conversation.

The intake process does require a significant amount of time for the church representative (typically, the special needs ministry coordinator). From personal experience, the person assigned with the role can expect to devote time to:

- Conducting the parent interview.

- Completing a write-up and formal intake document.

- Contacting assigned buddies and small group leaders who will play a part in the child's accommodation plan.

- Coaching the student's assigned buddies and teachers to help with the specific child's needs.

- Networking and introducing other relevant church leaders to family members.

Familiarity with special education or disability accommodation is helpful. While it is not necessary for the person conducting the parent interview to be credentialed, it is tremendously helpful for the person to be able to pick up on terms used by parents and to know where to interject important follow-up questions. (We'll walk you through the questions later in this chapter, helping interviewers who might not have a special needs background.)

Information gleaned from the intake conversation should be documented in a formal intake document. The interviewer should relay the learned information factually about the child. It is important to keep records where a family's dignity is preserved and where no assumptions or opinions are offered about a child or his or her family. The intake document should capture and convey information that wouldn't be received as an attempt to label a child or issue judgment for how parents are processing or addressing their child's disability.

A documented intake interview benefits everyone serving the child. Because of busy schedules and unexpected substitutes, there is rarely a time when every person involved in a child's accommodation plan can come together for a shared conversation. Excerpts from a documented intake interview can be provided to relevant volunteers, some of whom may be assigned as a last-minute substitute. (Let's face it, that's the real world in weekend church programming!) While guarding a family's privacy is extremely important, so, too, is the need to relay pertinent information to the child's leaders. Providing information from the intake interview ultimately helps the child's buddies and teachers better understand the participant with special needs. And familiarity with a child's specific strengths and weaknesses will enable the church leaders to exhibit patience while adapting lessons and encouraging peer interaction. For specific guidance on privacy protection, see the volunteer training topics in the appendix to chapter 7.

The signed intake form becomes part of the church's risk management policy. Following a standard intake process reduces potential problems and risks. Because issues are addressed in the intake interview about a child's medical needs, allergies, and behaviors, the church has the opportunity to prevent or appropriately respond to an undesirable situation.

In the summer of 2011, I included a child with autism in the five-year-olds class I was leading for my church's Vacation Bible School. I used the intake questionnaire (the same one provided at the end of this chapter) as a guide to interview the mother before the VBS week. During the conversation, the mother revealed that the child was prone to seizures and described a behavior that would surface as a warning just before a medical emergency. I asked several follow-up questions and then documented how our team could prevent injury and respond appropriately to that situation. Because the child's buddy (a responsible teen) had read the intake document I prepared, she responded beautifully when she recognized warning signs of a seizure. The buddy gently sat the child down on the ground and placed him in a position where he couldn't hit his head. Sure enough, the child had a seizure. And because of the buddy's response, our friend with special needs wasn't injured. The child went home early that day to recover but he was back in our VBS class first thing the next morning, ready to go.

Before the intake document is passed on to church leaders, require parents to review the document. Whenever I type out an intake document from the intake interview, I always send it back to the parents to make sure I've gotten it right. By providing parents the opportunity to see what is on file at the church, they have some control over what others are learning about their child. They can also correct any misperceptions or mistakes in the draft intake document. After the document is accurate and complete, parents return a signed copy to be on file with the church staff. Requiring parents to read and return a signed copy of their child's intake form prior to church participation serves several purposes:

- Permits parents to approve information being communicated about their child.

- Encourages parents to fully disclose their child's needs and abilities.

- Allows the church to adequately prepare for the child.

Sample Intake Form and Interview Guide

In the section that follows, I have created a sample intake form and explained the relevance of each question in the italics that follows. I've also provided some ideas for potential follow-up questions and noted what the interviewer is hoping to learn.

———

Parent Questionnaire for Children with Additional Needs

Our church cares for each participant inside our family ministry. The following questions are asked for the benefit of your child, so that we may provide the best experience and safest environment for everyone involved. Our church leaders and our ministry volunteers respect your family's right to privacy. Any information shared from this form is communicated directly with those caring for your child and only on a "need to know" basis. Please answer the below questions that apply to your child to help us serve your child better.

Form Completed by: *Name of church representative conducting and documenting the interview as well as name of person answering questions, usually a parent.*

Date: *Date the interview is completed*

Participant Name: *Child's name with additional needs*   **DOB:** *Child's date of birth*

Parent Contact: *Note parents' names, email addresses, cell phone numbers, etc. Aside from the need for emergency contact information, parents often love to get communication during the child's first day of participation. You may want to text a picture of the child doing something fun during church.*

Placement Notes: *Notes from interviewer with suggestions for placement. The special needs coordinator may need to consult with a children's pastor or other ministry leaders to select the best small group or assign the volunteer who is the* *best fit for this child's buddy or one-on-one aide. A particular class' schedule, the demeanor and teaching style of a volunteer leader, and other factors may all influence the placement of the child. And, the placement may change with some trial and error or the fluctuating needs of the child.*

My child has the following diagnosis, medical condition, or learning difference: *Obtaining the diagnosis for a child is not crucial to developing a successful plan for a child. But asking the question opens the door for more conversation. The more a parent will share about a child, the greater the likelihood of success. The goal of the conversation in this section is to learn about the child's specific needs and abilities as well as what has and has not worked in other settings for the child. And if the church representative conducting the interview is familiar with some common diagnoses, it may prompt them to ask additional and related questions.*

My child has the following allergies and/or food sensitivities: *Be sure to note if a child has the potential for an anaphylaxis type of reaction. Preparing for and reacting to a severe allergic reaction requires a different response than a food sensitivity or recommended diet.*

My child's main mode of functional communication is: *Find out how the child receives and communicates information. Some kids primarily learn through verbal or auditory means while others require all input visually. And some children are auditory learners yet struggle to communicate verbally themselves. This information can be very useful to a teacher who can adjust or modify a lesson to appeal to a child's particular learning style.*

The goals I have for my child's development this coming year include (behavioral, social, academic, etc.): *It isn't necessarily the church's goal to further a child's social or academic objectives. But the ministry team can learn a lot by asking this question of the parents. If Mom wants the child to try new things, then the church learns that the child is possibly more capable than he or she may appear. So, volunteers can make it a goal to gently nudge the child outside their comfort zone to participate in activities and interact with their peers. On the other hand, if Mom just wants the child to have a peaceful and enjoyable experience, then volunteers and buddies may not be so concerned about encouraging a child to do anything they don't want to do. This part of the conversation is* *likely to reveal a lot about the child's specific needs and capabilities. And while the church may not be able to achieve all of the parents' objectives, it really helps to know what the family's hopes are for the child. Church leaders can often do small things to help a child improve social skills and develop relationships with typically developing peers. In the church setting, a small group leader is already working to create interaction among everyone. So, incorporating a mother's goals, like this special education teach did, can be an easy and significant way to help a child.*

A public school teacher interviewed for this book shared a story that illustrates this point:

> "When I taught first grade in the public school system, my class included a boy named Lance.* Lance was a first-grader with Down syndrome. His mom wrote me a letter at the beginning of the year telling me how happy she was that he had me, and she really hoped he would develop lifelong friendships in my class. That helped me pair him better that year when we worked in small groups or when I chose his seating assignment. I picked kids that were patient and understanding, nurturers, and friendly to everyone. At the end of the year, Lance had two new best friends (Mary Claire and Elena) and he had been invited to his first typical play date. I didn't do anything outside of my teaching responsibilities, but I kept it in mind as I made instructional decisions in my classroom."
>
> *Names changed for privacy.*

My child has the following area(s) of interest: *Learning what a child loves is so important! Find out what the child enjoys doing, talking about, and excels in and then use these topics and activities to engage a child or to help them feel comfortable. Don't gloss over this question! Ask follow-up questions and expand on any insight the parents provide as to their child's loves and consider ways to develop success strategies from this information.*

It is not uncommon to learn that a child loves electronics. Be sure to ask about the use of electronics. Very often talking about or offering electronics in the church setting can be a problem if the child loves electronics so much that they

*can't stop once they start. Some kids fixate on electronics and struggle to partici-
pate in the environment once they see an iPhone, iPad, or similar device. Teen
buddies often need to be warned **not** to pull out their own iPhones and to stay off
the topic of video games when working alongside their friend with special needs.*

My child can do these things independently: *Be sure to find out if the child
can toilet independently. The church needs to determine how it will handle
diapering/toileting needs for children over a certain age (e.g., age four). You can
also use this question to learn more about what other activities the child needs
help with versus where they can be encouraged to do more on their own. Some
children may appear to need help doing certain activities (like a craft) when they
are capable of completing those exercises with less assistance.*

My child needs assistance with: *The parents may reveal that the child needs
help or a slower pace during specific times or activities in the children's ministry
setting. In the course of the conversation, the person interviewing the parent
should be asking questions to determine what type of assistance and what tools
work for the child when they are in need of help. Talk through each part of the
schedule (playtime, story time, music, worship, snack, craft, gross motor play,
transitions, small group, large group, peer interaction), prompting the parent to
share any specific needs or tips for success during each of these settings.*

My child is uncomfortable with or has an aversion to: *This is another
important question to address! Ask the parent how the child adjusts to transitions
and if there is anything the child is especially fearful of. Usually when this question is posed, the parent's memory will be jogged and he or she will share another
insightful tip for the ministry team. If the child struggles with new environments, change, and transitions, this is a time to start asking about the strategies
that work for that student. The church may offer to host a tour of the ministry
setting prior to Sunday morning programming or Vacation Bible School. Ask the
parents if providing a visual schedule or personal timer for the child would help
through transitions.*

**A trigger-point for resistance, frustration, or behavioral problems may
emerge for my child when:** *Behavior is a means of communication. Parents'
answers may reveal what a child may be trying to communicate when problematic behaviors surface. By asking the question, we can learn how to prevent and*

manage those problems before they start. Listening to the parents' response, we can get a feel for a number of issues that may affect the placement of a child. If a parent reveals that the child runs off as a way of expressing frustration, then ministry leaders may opt to place the child in a more secure, self-contained special needs environment since the risk of elopement is higher.

When/if my child experiences a period of frustration, he/she calms when we: *Getting this information is so important! Using calming strategies may keep an undesirable situation from turning into an unsafe situation.*

Doing/seeing/experiencing this one thing is an important part of my child's routine: *A few children may have something important in their routine that can be incorporated into the church setting.*

My child (circle one) does/does not enjoy music. *This is the time to find out how a child might react to participating in a worship experience. Often, a child will love to participate in music or worship so long as they have noise reduction earmuffs or another aid. Other children do better when the music is presented on a smaller scale and inside their own classroom, away from the lights, energy, and noise of a large group. For some kids, music may be their primary means for learning, and key to helping them develop spiritually.*

My child seems most relaxed in a setting (circle one): alone / with a few children / among many children *The interviewer may gain key insight from these answers and help with the placement or buddy pairing for the child.*

My child (circle one) would/would not enjoy a large group worship experience: *Many kids who struggle with inclusion in a typical small group setting may actually thrive in a typical large group setting. And the reverse is true for other kids who struggle with sensory overload. Large group worship and drama can be the source of great fun or tremendous frustration, depending on the child and the day!*

My child may be trying to communicate their need for (describe) _____ when he/she exhibits the following behavior. *Parents often reveal key insights when asked this question.*

My child is prone to seizures (circle one): YES / NO *Always ask this question. Learning the triggers and preventative measures for seizures for a specific child can be crucial.*

My child's behavior may indicate a medical problem requiring immediate attention when: *Again, asking questions and truly listening through the answer is likely to reveal some helpful pointers to a child's buddies and the children's ministry leadership team. Sometimes a child will exhibit a repetitive behavior or tic as a warning sign to a health problem.*

Other Information: *Note any additional information here.*

6. The Special Needs Ministry Leader

Successfully including students with special needs often requires a notable investment of time on the part of the church. Basic accommodation for a single child may necessitate multiple conversations to work through facility and logistical changes, volunteer coordination, and modifications to planned activities and curriculum. As a result, an increasing number of churches are recognizing the need to appoint a special needs ministry champion. I am often asked how to look for and hire the best person for this role on a church staff. And that's the reason we have this chapter. By and large, the special needs ministry leader is a translator of sorts, responsible for understanding and bridging the gap between two very unique cultures: the church and the special needs community.

Before I dive in, I want to share a little of my background and a couple of illustrations that will help as we continue in this chapter. Before I started writing on ministry issues I worked for a decade in the for-profit business world. And for some of that time I was a manufacturer's rep in the architectural interiors industry, selling large orders of custom furniture to corporations and educational institutions. When I started my job and with some regularity my manager spent time with me, learning about my personality and hearing about the projects I was managing. He did this with all the sales people who reported to him and he would use that knowledge as he assigned new sales accounts. He knew that if he correctly matched the personalities and skill-sets of each salesperson with the personalities and needs of each client, the odds of making a sale would improve. And that was good for all of us, because a single sale could sustain the salaries and jobs of many people, including workers in our company's manufacturing facilities. So it's from this starting point that we'll talk more about finding and hiring the right person to lead a church's special needs ministry.

Identify the Special Needs Ministry's "Clients"

When I sold orders of custom furniture, our sales cycles were long, sometimes lasting up to two years. During the months leading up to the sales decision, I was responsible for getting to know the work habits and personal preferences of my prospective clients. From there I would collaborate with my own company's product managers and industrial engineers to design a solution, tailored specifically to the needs of my client. My success was largely dependent on my ability to connect with my client and to adequately translate their needs into a solution that worked for them. I remember losing one of my first big sales opportunities after I failed to correctly identify my client. I had spent several months meeting with two particular employees from that client. But when the final decision was made, I learned there was another set of decision makers who had needs of their own that had never been considered. Not only did my proposal lack an appropriate solution addressing their needs, I had never made a connection with those individuals and frankly didn't know them at all. And people don't write big checks to people they don't know. So for nearly a year I didn't ask enough questions and I didn't realize that I wasn't developing a relationship nor designing a solution to meet the needs of half of the decision makers inside my client. To a large degree I wasted hours of time, and unfortunately my company lost out on a multi-million-dollar sales opportunity.

I share this story because over the past few years I have become increasingly aware of the fact few churches and ministry leaders accurately identify all the clients of the special needs ministry. As a result, management (church leadership) misses an opportunity to look for candidates with a skill-set that matches all, rather than just some, of the relevant decision makers. And what's worse, the new ministry leaders begin their job with an incomplete picture of whom they need to be developing a relationship with and the full scope of needs they should be designing accommodations around. So the special needs leader jumps right in, investing all their time in only some of their key decision makers and developing solutions that that meet only some of their clients' needs. It isn't long before that ministry leader hits a wall of fatigue and bewilderment because of wading through tension internal to the church every time they try to solve a problem or grow the ministry. Disillusioned, they attribute the problem to yet another case of the church "not getting it" and failing to support the special needs ministry. Another way of looking at it, as if the ministry leader can't quite "make the sale." But what the ministry leader doesn't understand is that they are like that salesperson named Amy Lee, who never identified all the decision markers on her big sales opportunity. In the case of the special needs ministry leader, their attempts to craft a solution or grow the ministry don't take into account all the clients and stakeholders to the ministry.

So who are the clients of the special needs ministry?

1. Individuals with special needs and their families.

Hip-hip-hooray, I know every reader correctly identified these client decision makers. It goes almost without saying that a special needs ministry leader is responsible for orchestrating care on behalf of the church for the individual with special needs and their family. In order to be successful, the ministry leader must have or quickly develop a deep level of appreciation for the special needs family. In order to design and implement ministry practices that meet the needs of this population, the leader should have familiarity with their common life experiences.

2. Volunteers serving the ministry.

We address the special needs ministry leader's relationship with the ministry's volunteers fairly extensively later in chapter 7, so I'll limit what I share here. But I'll go ahead and give you the punch line: when ministry leaders design the special needs ministry to simultaneously meet the needs of the volunteers, the special needs ministry can safely and successfully serve more individuals across a more diverse array of programs. A strong volunteer workforce is the fuel of every special needs ministry. It simply does not operate when the fuel runs out. So the ministry's success largely hinges on whether or not the volunteer has two big needs met: first, the ability to see how their contribution is making a meaningful impact in someone else's life; and second, experiencing a shared sense of community in their area of service. When a leader recognizes these needs and helps make them happen, more volunteers join the team, recruit friends to serve alongside them, and stay serving.

It is important to mention here that a strong special needs ministry leader will proactively set expectations for parents regarding what a ministry can and cannot do. This management of expectations is largely for the benefit of the volunteers. If an attitude of disappointment begins to eclipse an attitude of gratitude and if volunteers begin to feel that more is expected of them than they can appropriately offer, then the motivation for their service will evaporate instantly. And remember, volunteers want to feel they are changing someone's life for the better, not that they are failing to meet expectations. I'll stop on this note and invite you to learn more over in chapter 7.

3. The rest of the church staff.

Yes, I am in fact saying that the special needs ministry leaders' coworkers and peers *are also* clients of the ministry. Pause and read this again because it's big. The church staff running every other area of ministry inside the church is also a client of the special needs ministry. In my repeated observation, the ministry leaders that recognize their staff colleagues as their clients build more holistic special needs ministries. When the special needs ministry leader is building relationships across an entire church, the special needs ministry fuses into the DNA of the church. And when you find a special needs ministry leader who invests in the success of the children's pastor, the student pastor, and the worship pastor, and so on, you'll also find individuals with special needs who are embraced and included (sometimes with great ingenuity) in every crevice of that same church.

Unfortunately the church staff is the client that most special needs ministry leaders fail to recognize. Church leaders who interview candidates and ultimately hire their church's special needs leader often miss this as well. And so the new leader wasn't selected with the idea he or she needed to naturally care for and engage their staff peers. And because no one ever mentioned the idea that they were to help their peers succeed in their own respective ministries, the newly hired special needs ministry leader jumps into their role confused as to why their fresh ideas and accommodation solutions stall just as soon as they bump against another area of ministry. Going back to my personal illustration earlier in this chapter, it's as if the ministry leader doesn't understand why they can't make the sale and they aren't investigating the needs or developing a relationship with all clients of the ministry.

So how does this actually play out in the special needs ministry and church setting? Let me give you an example.

One ministry leader shares the story of having a teen with special needs that wanted to feel part of the church's student ministry. This individual had some physical disabilities and learning differences but was going through stages and life experiences common to every teen. He was asking good questions and beginning to develop an identity and faith of his own. He expressed a desire to meet one-on-one with the church's youth pastor. Like many students, he wanted this staff person to know his name and to know him personally. After some time, the special needs ministry leader became aware that connections and communications were being missed and this meeting between youth pastor and student kept not happening. The special needs ministry leader became frustrated that the pastor wasn't making this connection a priority. But before she gave up, got mad, or went to a higher-level staff person to complain, she reached out to the student pastor and asked him to meet with her. Because she had a relationship with the student pastor outside of this situation and had already gotten to know him personally along with his wife and kids, it was easy to start the conversation on a positive note. Within a few minutes the special needs leader recognized apprehension and anxiety on the part of the youth pastor. He was actually nervous about meeting this student with special needs. She restrained an understandable and natural inclination to judge her colleague and instead leaned into him, encouraging him and giving him confidence to do the next right thing. For the next few minutes she shared more about the teen, his abilities, his personality, and how he wanted to be known and have a place inside the student ministry. She provided valuable coaching for the youth pastor, giving him ideas for topics of conversation with the student and answering questions he had been embarrassed to ask on his own. It wasn't long after the two leaders met that the student pastor sat down with the teen with special needs. The pastor and the student with special needs left their scheduled time together with a sense of accomplishment.

Do you see what happened here? The special needs ministry leader had a relationship with the youth pastor so when the signs of a problem emerged, she already had an established rapport. There was enough shared trust to begin a conversation from a positive point of view and broach a difficult subject. And when everyone began to realize a problem had emerged, the actions of the special needs ministry leader kept the situation from spiraling to the point of no return. The special needs ministry leader wasn't just concerned with the success of her teen with special needs; she wanted her pastor friend to succeed too!

Let's think about the wins out of this situation. Before you proceed in reading further, I'd challenge you to set the book down a few moments and make some notes.

Do you see a trickle-down effect from the shared conversation between ministry leaders?

Who are the beneficiaries of that conversation?

How does the way this situation was handled affect the teen today and one year from today?

What are some possible outcomes that could have resulted without the meeting between the two leaders?

How does this leader conversation have a broader impact on the special needs ministry?

How does this leader conversation have a broader impact on the student ministry?

Do you anticipate the student ministry leader would approach the special needs leader again with questions?

Good Team Players Make Good Ministry Leaders

Special needs ministry should never be an isolated ministry. If it ever becomes that, then hit the pause button and start asking questions. If a ministry leader senses he/she or the entire ministry is functioning like a separate, satellite ministry rather than as an integrated ministry of the church, then I would challenge the leader to begin looking for ways he or she can serve the leaders of other ministries. If a special needs ministry leader isn't thinking about the holistic mission of the church and how every ministry needs to succeed, we've probably found at least part of the reason why the special needs ministry is sitting off in a corner all by itself. The ministry leaders who are good team players on a church's staff tend to build better ministries of their own. Why? Because they play nice and care about the well-being of others. And everybody wants friends like that. These ideas and principles are true for every area of ministry, not just special needs. Goodness, as I type these words my mind is flooding with examples of good and bad team players I've encountered on a church's staff over the years. As the daughter of a senior pastor, I grew up watching my dad manage ministry leaders. He didn't have to open up a personnel file for me to figure out which staff members were better team players. Sometimes I knew because those were the same staff members who got to know me as the daughter of one of their co-workers. And through their actions, they showed that they cared about their co-workers child—me. Many of the staff members and co-workers of my father are active in my life today, still caring about me and in fact cheering me on as I write this book.

In the business world there is a term often used to describe a type of transaction or sale where a business sells to another business and where the benefitting consumer is not directly involved, it's called "business to business." In many cases, special needs ministry is a "business to business" ministry. The ministry exists to support other ministries and to help them successfully include the individual with special needs. When full inclusion is happening successfully, the work of the special needs ministry may be invisible to many people including the individual with special needs, much like the role of a business-to-business entity is invisible to the end consumer. I benefit from the work of business-to-business companies because I buy produce almost daily that has been transported and brokered by a business in between the farm that grew the fruits and vegetables and the grocery store that sells it to me. Much like the produce wholesaler, the special needs ministry is the behind-the-scenes mechanism that allows individuals with special needs to participate in all their regular ministry environments. What follows is a task list that a special needs ministry leader might follow (or delegate) in a scenario where a student is fully included under the umbrella of another ministry and where the special needs ministry's role is behind the scenes and somewhat invisible:

- Conduct intake interview with parents to become acquainted with the student with unique needs.

- Contact the ministry leader over the student's age/stage of life (e.g., children's pastor, student pastor, etc.). Share "need to know" information about the new student. Collaborate with that ministry leader to determine which small group is the best fit for the particular individual.

- Contact the assigned small group leader and provide coaching to help them experience success with the student. Share ideas on how to help the student feel comfortable, how to address differences with the typical peers, and how to address any unexpected or undesirable behaviors that might surface and that the parents mentioned in the intake interview.

- Contact the student ministry leader to follow up on a reference check on two new applicants to be teen buddies. Discuss their personalities and gifts with the student ministry leader to determine which would be the best match for the new participant with special needs.

- Schedule and walk the new buddy through a special needs buddy training.

- Prepare a customized visual schedule, church map, and/or reward chart for teen buddy to use with the new student with special needs.

- Schedule and host a practice walk-through and church tour for the new student with special needs and their family.

- Periodically check in with the individual and/or their parents, the student's buddy, and volunteers serving the student. Address any concerns or make necessary adjustments to the student's accommodation plan.

When you read through this task list, can you see where staff leaders and participants from other church ministries are also clients of the ministry? A good special needs leader is completing our example task list with a desire to help each person involved experience success.

Volunteer or Paid?

As churches correctly recognize the need for a single person to take ownership of the special needs ministry, many wonder if a volunteer can fulfill this role. Personally, I am not a fan of using unpaid volunteers to lead the ministry and for several reasons. For starters, not paying someone to work in a pastoral leader role nearly always creates an unhealthy dynamic between the unpaid leader and the other church staff leaders who are paid. In those situations it is easy for a superiority or inferiorly complex to emerge somewhere in the co-workers' relationships. If, however, the senior leaders on the church staff are bi-vocational and/or unpaid, then there is a strong case for asking a person inside the church to pray about leading the special needs ministry in an unpaid capacity. But when a church's executive team, who receive fair compensation packages themselves, asks someone to run the ministry in an unpaid or significantly underpaid capacity, they are essentially saying "your work is not as valuable as my work." The Bible has quite a bit to say about paying a worker a fair wage and the wages he is due. And I wonder about the biblical basis of a decision when I hear about a church with a large staff of full-time ministry leaders that turns down a request to create a paid staff position to lead the special needs ministry. I have grieved to see some very respected churches turn down such a request, especially after a volunteer has invested years of emotional and physical energy building that church's special needs ministry.

There are other reasons I believe it is wise for the special needs leader position to be a formal and paid staff position. If the ministry-leader role is fulfilled by an unpaid volunteer, it is unlikely they are included in staff meetings or leadership-level conversations. And that can cause problems of its own because the person leading the ministry doesn't have the opportunity to see all the mechanisms of the church at play and from a broader perspective. If that leader is never exposed to staff meetings and big-picture conversations, they don't have context to understand things like why their budget was cut or how a church decision is affecting other ministries and not just special needs. Without being exposed to those big-picture conversations, the special needs ministry leader is more likely to take things personally and feel that the special needs ministry is either forgotten or isolated.

In addition, an unpaid employee is less likely to provide a consistent level of ownership in the ministry, and there are often risk management implications when that happens. I can remember interviewing a volunteer ministry leader several years ago that shared how she preferred remaining in an unpaid position because she didn't want to follow all the procedures and do some of the administrative tasks the church had asked her to do. And she went on to share how she didn't use the church's intake interview process, preferring instead to "wing it" when new participants arrived with special needs. Sometimes that approach works just fine. But it never works all of the time. And it didn't work all of the time for that church, which has since hired someone else to lead the special needs ministry in a more defined and accountable role.

Last, it is very difficult for a church to give any sort of constructive feedback to an unpaid worker. Job performance reviews just don't work the same for volunteers as they do for paid positions. And in those times when the special needs ministry and/or leader can benefit from constructive feedback (and that will happen!), it's all but impossible to go down that path if the ministry's leader is serving in a strictly volunteer, unpaid capacity.

Effective Leaders Are Skilled Diplomats

Before we move on, I want to close this section by pointing to the fact that the most effective special needs ministry leaders are creative problem-solvers and skilled diplomats. Developing each ministry participant's individualized accommodation plans and within the resource limitations of a church is not always easy. Many situations require an abundance of discernment. In addition, some parents come to church with the same advocating mind-set they use inside their child's public school. While this is understandable, it is rarely enjoyable to be on the receiving end of such an approach. The best ministry leaders know to expect these encounters and they don't take it personally or get rattled when a family member's emotions, often already close to the surface, escape and occasionally become misdirected. It is for these reasons the person best suited for the role is someone with a strong sense of self-awareness, emotional stability, and spiritual maturity.

I've been asked for a job description for a special needs ministry leader on numerous occasions. A few years ago I typed out the following sample job description for a requesting church. I've decided to include it in this book. However, this is long and probably not practical to be used as the official job description kept on file. I suggest you pull some ideas and create a more concise job description that fits the culture and needs of your church.

Sample Job Description for Special Needs Ministry Leader

Optional titles: Pastor of Special Needs, Staff Leader for Special Needs, Special Needs Ministry Director, Inclusion Coordinator, Special Needs Champion

By using the gifts of leadership, administration, and communication, this person will serve as the central contact point and conduit between the church staff and families requiring special accommodation. The ability of the special needs ministry leader to problem-solve is crucial in order to enable a successful church experience for children and families impacted by many types of special needs, including but not limited to learning differences, intellectual disability, and unique physical needs. While many details and duties associated with this role are administrative, the position is a ministerial role with expectations in line with 1 Timothy 3.

Through each of the gifts and skill-sets listed below, this person will have the following job responsibilities:

Leadership Skills

Develop a vision and specific goals for the special needs ministry. Work with the church's senior leaders to make sure the ideas and action steps are complimentary to the church's other goals and available resources. Help senior leaders craft their own vision for the church with disability inclusion in mind.

Determine the short-term and long-term programming objectives for the ministry. Items to consider include services and/or times when special needs accommodations and classrooms will be available; whether or not the church will offer special needs accommodation during VBS and Wednesday night programming; and what additional events and services the ministry will offer, such as parent support groups, respite events, or outreach events.

Support other church staff members and key ministry leaders. Meet with ministry peers such as the pastor to students and pastor to children. Determine how other leaders and volunteers serving in other areas of ministry can benefit from training or one-on-one conversations to work through accommodation challenges.

Establish a process for assessing needs of ministry participants. Develop accommodation plans from completed intake interviews or assessment conversations.

Consider how individuals with special needs can best be included and experience meaningful spiritual growth of their own. Design a plan for volunteer or peer buddies while considering what specially tailored ministry environments may be needed. Ages and ability levels of ministry participants will determine the type and number of accommodation options needed.

Recruit ministry volunteers. Determine the best way to publicize the need for volunteers and attract people to serve in the ministry.

Develop volunteer roles. Write job descriptions and expectations to help prospective and new volunteers understand how they can help and what defines success. Consider setting up buddy or assistant rotations. Consult other ministry leaders as needed (e.g., using teen volunteers also involved in the church's student ministry).

Offer regular volunteer training. Offer ideas for adapting teaching for special needs and cover topics such as those featured in the appendix 7 pieces at the back of the book.

Inform senior church leaders of any new developments related to special needs that may affect the church. Trends and best practices from other churches or from the medical or education field may be relevant to the church from time to time. In addition, new products or legal issues could be of interest to a church's executive staff.

Develop a special needs addendum to the preschool and children's ministry handbooks. Any policies and practices developed with special needs in mind should complement the other ministries and should be applied in a way to avoid the practice or perception of discrimination (e.g., behavioral guidelines consistently applied to participants regardless of disability).

Select or modify curriculum so that participants can engage in Bible lessons. It is important to note that selecting and certainly writing or modifying curriculum for individuals with special needs draws from a different skillset than the other leadership responsibilities listed here. Creating engaging Bible stories and activities or modifying existing curriculum often requires familiarity with special education practices and can also be very time consuming. As a result, a person other than the day-to-day special needs ministry leader may take on the responsibility of finding or creating accessible Bible lessons.

Administration Skills

Create and update participant profiles. Complete the registration documents and/or intake interview process with new ministry participants. Update annually and as-needed.

Oversee volunteer application process. Conduct interview and complete background check with new volunteers.

Maintain ministry records. Create and update database of all ministry participants and volunteers. Maintain and post current schedule of volunteers.

Create and file documentation as behavior challenges and safety concerns arise.

Draft an annual ministry budget. Follow approved budget.

Communication Skills

Initiate regular ministry updates and reminders through relevant communication means. Utilize email, texts, and social media to communicate with and facilitate conversation between ministry participants and volunteers.

Networking Skills

Develop relationships with leaders of other ministries inside the church. The ability of the special needs ministry leader to forge trust and friendship with other church leaders will enable greater awareness for the special needs ministry, easier volunteer recruitment, and opportunities for partnering in events and programming.

Develop relationships with key contacts outside the church. At some point in time every church benefits from a consultative conversation with an expert, oftentimes from the field of education, medicine, mental health, or the legal profession. And a special needs ministry leader will be a better leader by having positive and supportive relationships with the leaders of nearby churches also doing (or wanting to do) special needs ministry. In addition, a leader who has good relationships throughout the community will often find people who have a heart and passion for working with individuals with special needs but who do not currently attend a church. Some of the best special needs volunteers are often unchurched people who just need a reason to get involved in a church that offers service opportunities matching their gifts and interests.

Team Player

Recognize, proactively communicate with, and work through accommodation challenges with other impacted ministries. The ability to work well with staff peers in other areas of ministry is crucial for the success of the special needs ministry. Similarly, a special needs ministry leader who identifies opportunities to partner with and support other church ministries will increase the effectiveness of the ministry while contributing to the overarching goals of the church.

It is especially important for a special needs ministry leader to develop a strong relationship with the preschool, children's, and student ministry teams. The role of the special needs ministry champion is to facilitate the success of the participant with special needs and to *support* the ministry leader in the respective area of participation. For example, the special needs ministry leader is responsible for collecting relevant information about the first grader who has been identified with Aspergers syndrome. The special needs ministry leader is then responsible for initiating a partnership with the children's ministry leader to develop the child's accommodation plan. Both leaders should respect the other's insight, experience, and volunteer relationships. The same would be true when facilitating inclusion for the individuals of other ages inside their respective age-appropriate ministries.

Judgment/Spiritual Maturity

Make decisions and conduct one's self in accordance with the New Testament principles for leaders in the church. Because of the unique needs and individual-specific nature of special needs ministry, the special needs ministry leader can anticipate conversations that require the highest level of diplomacy. The ability to convey difficult messages in love and with respect for the church's leadership is imperative. It is not always possible for the church to meet the desires of every family. And as a representative of Jesus and of the employing church, it is the job of the special needs ministry leader to sometimes make relationally difficult decisions and to relay those decisions back to a family. And while the central responsibility of a special needs ministry leader is to enable accommodation for every family, all decisions must be executed through the lens of Scripture and with the goal of doing what is best for the larger body of the church.

Bonus Skills

Ideally, a special needs ministry leader is familiar with the vernacular and culture of the special needs and disability world. It is extremely helpful for this person to have working knowledge of current terms used in special education, pediatric therapies, and medical fields that pertain to special education and various neurological and physical diagnoses. Because parents will sometimes not disclose all relevant facts to church representatives, it is very helpful for the person interviewing parents or new participants to have a working knowledge of special needs terms and phrases. Parents often use these terms or words in the course of conversation and certain words may indicate an increased need for specialized accommodation. In addition, by being familiar with references, the ministry leader conducting the intake interview may recognize the need to resource the appropriate specialists or experts as they develop a child's accommodation plan. Last, it is very helpful for a special needs champion to have some familiarity with current practices in local school systems, especially where risk management is concerned.

A Closing Note Regarding This Job Description

Rarely is there one single person who possesses all the skills or has the availability to achieve every task we've listed. It is common to see a church pair two or more people with complementing skill-sets to coordinate different aspects of the special needs ministry. Perhaps your church has a special education professional that already has a weekday job, but has availability to conduct parent interviews, give advisement for individual accommodation plans, or provide regular counsel the ministry leaders. Or maybe your church has a person skilled with administrative gifts who can help with the tasks requiring those skills.

7. Volunteers: Leading, Recruiting, Training, and Creating Community

W e know that without the help of volunteers, special needs inclusion and accommodation is virtually impossible. The churches with the strongest special needs ministries seem to know the secret: *a ministry leader who values their relationships with their volunteers almost as much as they value their relationships with the families they serve.* Time and again, I have found that behind every thriving ministry is a leader who lives out the love of Christ through their personal connection with the ministry's volunteers. And that care and attention spills over into the relationships between the volunteers and the families the ministry serves. Let me illustrate this through my own experience with some of these special needs leaders.

In the introduction to Section 2, I shared some details about my research for this book. As I was thinking about people I should acknowledge, I sat down with a pen and paper attempting to recount every church leader who had obliged me with an interview or helped to answer reader questions from my blog. Within five minutes, I had written down more than fifty names. Without a doubt I didn't recall every person who had helped me. But as I studied my scribbled list of recalled names, I realized that many had since become genuine and cherished friends of mine. I don't think I knew any of the ministry leaders prior to contacting them for help regarding special needs ministry. But, over the course of the last few years, many of these leaders have become close personal friends. These are the people who have remembered my birthday, who have prayed for me when life has thrown a couple of lemons my way, who have graciously listened to me whine when the online world was a little cruel, and who have made me laugh until my sides hurt. These are ladies (yes, the vast majority are indeed women) who have endeared themselves to me personally and whom I have truly grown to love and appreciate.

And guess what else these ladies have in common? These very same people are directing ministries with the largest and most cohesive volunteer bases. In many cases, I have actually visited their churches or connected with those who serve alongside them. And every time, without fail, I discover that my experience with these ladies is the very same experience their volunteers have with them. The people serving around them feel loved and valued as human beings, not just for what they offer their ministry. And the volunteers and coworkers all echo a genuine enjoyment whenever they are around this ministry leader. Each of these ministry leaders has a gift for making life and serving fun. That's not to say these ladies don't have some grit! Whoa, do they! In fact, their willingness to get a bit feisty is one of the main reasons they are so loved.

Creating Community

The importance of creating community inside the special needs ministry can't be overstated or emphasized enough if you want to create a rapidly multiplying volunteer base while fostering a healthy ministry environment. When you nurture and prioritize relationship for the volunteers, the volunteers become the ministry's greatest recruiting tool, because *they tell others.* Word of mouth is especially important for Millenials, the generation our churches are becoming increasingly dependent on for volunteers. This generation, comprised of

> Everyone craves connection and a sense of purpose. Whenever a church leader can facilitate a ministry environment that fulfills those needs in volunteers, there is a win for everyone.

individuals in their late teens to mid-thirties, prefers to donate their time to organizations and causes that they learn about from a friend.[1] These ministry workers value a personal invitation over a well-produced marketing campaign. And that's good news for special needs ministries that don't have big budgets for publicity videos or the opportunity to receive promotion from the pulpit. As soon as Millennial-aged volunteers get involved in a place they feel they are making a difference and developing meaningful relationships, they do something naturally. They tell their friends about their positive experience. And because those friends want that same taste of purpose and connection, they sign up to help too. This positive experience cycle repeats itself and the ministry's volunteer base multiplies organically.

> Stonebriar Community Church in Frisco, Texas, has a waiting list of volunteers. Yes, you read that correctly. This church serves approximately one hundred families of children with special needs. And incredibly, there are more people wanting to serve these families than there are spots inside the ministry. Through several visits to this church campus and interviews with their leaders, I experienced firsthand what was driving the desire to serve inside this ministry; it was a strong sense of community among the volunteers. In an interview with Meaghan Wall, the Staff Pastoral Leader of Special Needs for Stonebriar Community Church, Meaghan shared a story that perhaps best captures the simple yet profound ways a leader can foster a sense of community inside the ministry and for the volunteers.
>
> Meaghan remembered that, not long after she began leading the special needs ministry, one of the volunteers had just experienced a devastating loss, the untimely death of her brother. Meaghan contacted the volunteer to see if there was any way she could offer support. The volunteer, who was in shock and grief, could only think of or put into words a concern over what she would pack for her work lunch the next day. Meaghan told the volunteer not to worry and it would be taken care of. Within hours, Meaghan was at this lady's doorstep with a sack of groceries. And this lady was able to pack her next day's lunch with items on her special diet. Meaghan explained that years after her crisis, this volunteer would still recall with emotion and

gratitude how she was ministered to through the delivery of a small sack of groceries. This volunteer has through the years remained fiercely loyal to the special needs ministry largely because she was served by its community during a time of her own need.

I heard similar stories from other churches with a strong special needs ministry.

One church leader shared that a special needs ministry volunteer began calling in sick with greater frequency. The leader wondered if this helper wasn't taking her commitment to serve seriously. Rather than assume too much, the church leader invited the volunteer to meet for coffee. The leader then learned that the volunteer was in an abusive relationship that was behind the sudden absences. The church leader took this knowledge and immediately called in support for the volunteer from other ministries inside the church. So instead of "firing" the volunteer over coffee, the leader stepped into her life and widened her community. The volunteer welcomed the offer to receive valuable coaching from other church ministries. And she went on to experience meaningful life change. Now, a few years removed from the spell of absences and the coffee shop conversation, the same volunteer shows up faithfully in the special needs ministry. But that isn't all. This volunteer is now a lay care ministry leader in the church's Stephen Ministry.[2]

It shouldn't surprise you that this situation happened inside a church that benefits from a mind-boggling number of volunteers that sustain Sunday morning programming across multiple campuses, recurring respite events, parent support group meetings, and overnight retreat experiences for kids with special needs.

Reflecting on these stories, do you see the connection between a ministry that gives their volunteers a story of their own to share with friends and a ministry that can successfully recruit a whole bunch of volunteers?

On their own, the leader of a church's special needs ministry can't meet every need of every volunteer or participating family. But that leader can model service in a way that caring becomes contagious. And that leader can also assign volunteer support roles to other volunteers who naturally engage and enjoy connecting with colleagues inside the ministry. Perhaps one of the easiest ways to foster a sense of community is for the leader to invite an appropriately gifted volunteer to share ownership in the volunteer support role for the ministry. Many ministry servants have the gift of hospitality. And like most volunteers, they are happiest when they are using their natural talents in the context of ministry. Volunteers with the gifts of hospitality and administration may find it rewarding to coordinate meals, plan a baby or bridal shower, order a "Congratulations Graduate!" banner, or write short notes of encouragement, all in support of fellow ministry helpers. Community-building tasks are often the most fun "chores" to assign volunteers. And nearly always these things can be accomplished from home, on virtually any time schedule, and through online communications.

Leadership and Volunteer Attraction

One observation that seems to come up often through my leader interviews and church visits is that well-run ministries tend to naturally attract strong volunteers. The great news is that for thriving ministries with solid leaders, volunteer recruitment is more about attraction than a convincing sales pitch. Jim Wideman is a longtime children's pastor, author, coach, and conference speaker.[3] Jim often talks about the fact that a ministry's best volunteer is only as good as the ministry's leader. That kind of statement makes us leaders squirm a little, doesn't it? But it doesn't have to. Being a good leader is something we can all strive toward—being dependable, following through, and communicating in a timely manner. When we do these things, we're rewarded with a team of reliable and relational ministry volunteers.

> Volunteer recruitment is more about attraction than a convincing sales pitch.

People don't expect perfection, but they do appreciate when they see leaders who sincerely try to improve and ask for help in areas where they might be weak. You don't have to be good at everything to lead, but the best leaders are honest about where they need assistance, working to fill in those gaps, while also taking action and responsibility for areas of personal growth. I've volunteered under a leader who lacked a strong work ethic and rarely responded when I asked for assistance. And you know what I eventually did? Yep, I quit! I found another area of ministry where the leader appreciated my contribution, had genuine interest in the success of the ministry, and who carried their fair share of the weight with the workload. Because most ministry workers aren't paid, they have no incentive to stay and serve if things are disorganized and dysfunctional. People aren't usually looking for more to do; but they are looking for opportunities where what they do matters and changes things for the better.

A great book to read (or find summary notes on) is Daniel Pink's book, *Drive: The Surprising Truth about What Motivates Us* (New York: Penguin, 2009). I can sum up Pink's research simply by saying that volunteers are most motivated when their leader gives them a MAP. In this acronym, "M" stands for *mastery*—meaning volunteers want to get better at what they do, so they'd like multiple opportunities and ways to receive training and learn new skills. "A" stands for *autonomy*—meaning volunteers appreciate having choices when they serve and gain confidence when they're given responsibility and more ownership in things that really matter in the ministry. And "P" stands for *purpose*—meaning volunteers want to be part of something that's bigger than themselves, they long to make a real difference in the world. We'll talk more about training and offering choices to volunteers in the appendix pages to this chapter.

On a personal level, I also think about volunteers and retaining them through a parent's perspective. Mamas don't like to leave their babies in rooms of people that appear unsafe or unfriendly (and I use the term "babies" in a broad sense here. . . . I still refer to my elementary-aged son as my "baby" at times). As a longtime children's ministry volunteer and a mom, I've both resigned my volunteer service and withdrawn my child from a ministry environment where the overseeing staff member didn't seem to take their job or the volunteers' responsibilities seriously. In contrast, and without any begging, I've been excited to serve in ministry environments where leaders carried themselves professionally. Their leadership was contagious, and as a result the entire ministry rose to the leader's level of professionalism.

A leader who demonstrates a personal commitment and enthusiasm for the ministry is much more likely to draw like-minded volunteers who are themselves sacrificially committed. Fortunately, I have yet to meet a special needs ministry leader who wasn't both committed to the ministry and remarkably likable. In fact, every special needs minister I've ever interviewed was a skilled problem solver (that seems to be the most important and necessary attribute for not only surviving but thriving in ministry). My intuition tells me that by its very nature, special needs ministry tends to attract a more competent and passionate person to leadership.

Give the Ministry Visibility

Many of the churches with thriving special needs ministries effectively spotlight the ministry inside the worship center (stay tuned for some related ideas). These occasions nearly always provide a huge boost to the volunteer base, with a flurry of interest from prospective ministry servants. During a weekend worship service, a video may be shown with clips of students with special needs participating in the church environment. The video might also incorporate personal stories, allowing the church to see how the ministry has touched the spiritual journey of a family or even a volunteer serving in the ministry. Some churches may also feature a live interview from the stage of parents of a child with special needs or of the special needs ministry leader. While it is not necessary for the church's lead pastor to publicly endorse the ministry, it is a huge opportunity to influence the growth of the ministry and shape the church culture when he does so. A pastor can have a tremendous influence on a church by celebrating the blessings of the special needs ministry.

> A pastor can have a tremendous influence on a church by celebrating the blessings of the special needs ministry.

Some churches devote a designated weekend to being a "special needs emphasis Sunday." If you ask church members at Stonebriar Community Church in Frisco, Texas, which is their favorite Sunday of the year, odds are you'll hear about their dedicated special needs service more than a few times. Preparation for this annual Sunday begins weeks in advance, when a photographer comes to the church to snap professional shots of every family participating in the special needs ministry. By having the church select and provide the photographer, there is consistency in the photos and families can come to a familiar place where the child with special needs feels comfortable. For many families, this photo shoot may be the first or only time they have done a professional photo sitting. Often, parents fear their child with special needs would not participate as expected and so they never even try for a real family photo. The photographer follows the families, snapping numerous pictures while allowing the children to select where they will sit and how long the session will last. The photographer captures natural moments, allowing the photo shoot to be fun rather than a tug-of-war. One photo of each family is provided for free to the parents and is also featured in the emphasis Sunday video. In addition, the church enlarges many of the photographs and displays a family photo wall in the entrance to the church's special needs ministry suite. I've seen this photo wall in person. And, it's pretty hard not to feel tremendous emotion when seeing portraits of God's handiwork!

In addition to featuring a video about the ministry, Stonebriar Community Church's pastor, Chuck Swindoll, interviews the special needs ministry leader during the service. Their leader, Meaghan Wall, may highlight one or two ministry "wins" from the past year and then talk about what's on the horizon for the coming year. Then, the entire service involves ministry participants in one way or another. On that Sunday, children and adults who participate in the ministry can be observed:

1. Greeting worshipers and handing out the bulletins.

2. Serving alongside ushers, receiving the offering.

3. Reciting Scripture during the service (one student or adult is selected for this role).

4. Singing on stage for the special music.

5. Collecting an "exit offering" as worshipers leave church, which is designated for the special needs family camp the ministry participates in each summer.

Possibly the greatest outcome from the impact Sunday is that it makes individuals with special needs a visible part of the body of Christ. And after this Sunday, the average churchgoer has something to talk about when they pass a child or family in the hallway that was featured in the church service. Showing participants in a positive light may be the first time some parents have had their child celebrated at all, let alone publicly. The church cannot underestimate the meaningful way this affects a family of a child with special needs. Using the public venue of a worship service will shape the entire church's view of disability, reminding them of God's value for everyone.

There is another benefit to spotlighting the special needs ministry that I want to share and not have misinterpreted—namely, fundraising. One temptation might be to say that the primary purpose of promoting the special needs ministry publicly is all about raising money, and it isn't. But for those churches that worry about the costs of a ministry, this story is to show that when you are faithful, God does provide.

> When I first started writing on the topic of church inclusion, a senior pastor privately shared a story with me. Shortly after the church spotlighted their new special needs ministry in a worship service, they received an unexpected financial blessing. A nondescript but regularly attending church member made an appointment to meet with the pastor. In the meeting, this member shared that he had been the parent of a child with special needs years before the pastor had come to this church. While the child was no longer living, the memories of the child and the family's experience were still fresh. This father was touched by the church's initiative to better include kids with special needs, and he wanted to see the new ministry succeed. While he wasn't in a place where he could serve as a caregiver, he had the financial means to make a contribution. Before the church member left the pastor's office he pulled out a large check. A designated gift was made that day for the purpose of sustaining the ministry, especially through its early years. The church then outfitted a room with a few pieces of sensory equipment and created a new staff position to coordinate the weekly details of the special needs ministry.

Recruiting Volunteers

Especially when the ministry is first starting and before a leader has had the opportunity to establish a rapport and reputation, volunteer recruitment is a top priority. What follows is a short "brainstorming" session of sorts, sharing various ideas for finding new volunteers.

Participate in ministry fairs. Ensure the special needs ministry has a presence at the church ministry fairs or any type of event where service opportunities inside the church are explained and publicized. The church website, emails, and newsletters also present great opportunities to feature the stories of participants and blessings of the volunteers.

Partner with a local university. Several church leaders have developed relationships with the faculty of nearby colleges or seminaries. Often when a school's administration becomes familiar with a church's special needs ministry, they will encourage or even create incentives for their students to volunteer. For students pursuing degrees in social work, counseling, early childhood education, or family ministry, this experience is tremendously valuable, making the student volunteers better job candidates to prospective employers. And often, these same students do a great job working alongside individuals with special needs.

Promote the ministry through a publicity tour of adult small groups and other ministry meetings. Personally visiting smaller venues inside the church is a great way to talk about special needs inclusion and engage people who might not otherwise be aware of the ministry. The most effective volunteer recruitment happens through one-on-one interactions and relationships. Collaborating with other church leaders and figuring out ways for two ministries to work together is usually a win for everyone involved. Perhaps the special needs ministry will work with the church's benevolence ministry to host a food drive or a coat collection. Several churches have a formal plan for how their care ministry (e.g., Stephen Ministry) can partner with the special needs ministry to assist families. It is important to note that one of the most important jobs of the special needs ministry leader is to be the public cheerleader for the ministry. Getting out into the church and giving a face to the ministry will ultimately facilitate more interactions where people can learn about the ministry.

> One of the most important jobs of the special needs ministry leader is to be the public cheerleader for the ministry.

Offer one-time service opportunities. People are generally less reticent to help if they can have a commitment-free opportunity to "test drive" their service with the special needs ministry. Asking an adult small group to provide the volunteers for a single occasion, such as putting on an Easter egg hunt for the ministry, hosting the Christmas party, or even staffing a one-time parents' night out (respite event) may be more palatable to churchgoers who are initially reluctant to make a long-term service commitment. According to the 2014 Millennial Impact Project, Millenials (individuals born between 1980 and 2000) prefer to help a cause or nonprofit in shorter volunteer stints before committing larger increments of time. The research also shows that this same group of volunteers is more likely to return and commit to more volunteer time if they feel like they can bring change for someone or tangibly help someone's life for the better. Millenials want to see how their one or two hours of service can make a difference. In my opinion, that's an easy homerun for a church's special needs ministry! Once people gain comfort and confidence around individuals with special needs, they often experience the call for regular service soon after. In addition, finding ways to expose future volunteers to the ministry outside of just providing childcare may ease any apprehensions. For example, asking a gifted artist to design the ministry logo, inviting a hobby photographer to take pictures at a ministry event, requesting a social media expert to set up and help administer social networking accounts on behalf of the ministry, or asking a musician to play their instrument inside the ministry environment, are all ways to engage new people in the ministry. For a list of ideas of one-time service opportunities, see appendix 7.4.

> People are generally less reticent to help if they can have a commitment-free opportunity to "test drive" their service with the special needs ministry.

Make it meaningful. God created humans in His image, and so like our Creator, people are wired to love and help others. While we may not always do those things well, secular studies support this notion. In his best-selling book, *Give and Take: a Revolutionary Approach to Success*, organizational psychology professor Adam Grant shares the findings of his own research that people want to be of service and contribute to the lives of others. Grant's studies show that the single biggest motivator for increased productivity in the workplace is for a person to find meaning and purpose in their job. And they want to know that what they do in their job matters.[4]

This core human need for meaning and contribution provides a unique opportunity for a church's special needs ministry. Where else can someone serve and see a comparable return on investment of their time and talent? The impact and benefit is immediate to the person with a disability or their entire family. I am reminded of the volunteer storyteller I met a couple of years ago while visiting a church in Northern California.

> On this particular Sunday I was the guest of the leader who had helped to start the church's special needs ministry nearly twenty years earlier. She introduced me to various small group leaders and buddies who were assisting children with special needs as they attended their regular grade-level small groups and so forth. This special needs ministry leader had me all over the campus, observing different groups and classes where individuals with disability were actively participating. It was a joy to see all the places special needs ministry was happening throughout the church. But I will never forget my experience in the class with the individuals with the most significant disabilities. The participants in this group were young adults who were nearly all difficult to understand, had severe intellectual disability, and who exhibited "challenging" behaviors on a recurring basis. As best I can recollect, several of the students required some form of physical assistance as well. To me, this was a difficult crowd. I can remember walking in the room and wondering how hard it had to be to recruit volunteers to serve this environment. I'm sure God heard my thoughts and decided to address them immediately because it wasn't minutes before I observed perhaps the most gifted, animated, and engaging volunteer worker I'd ever seen in a special needs ministry setting.
>
> Shortly after these students with significant special needs completed their opening activities, the class storyteller then arrived. Immediately recognizing this nice-looking man, aged in his mid-fifties, the class participants moved with surprising ease and anticipation to hear the Bible story. With delight, the volunteer storyteller greeted each individual by name. He then pulled out a visual board

with symbols and invited the students to choose a song. Without skipping a beat, they pointed to a selected symbol and all participated in praise worship in some way. The storyteller then involved the students in the Bible story and successfully held their attention the entire time he had the floor. And when he asked questions tailored to their abilities, the students pointed to symbols, nodded, and made various gestures to indicate they had learned from his Bible lesson. During prayer time the volunteer offered pictures of fellow group members. The participants selected and held visual reminders as they were led to pray for one another. I watched all of this in utter amazement. It had only been minutes earlier that the same students labored to move from one chair to another and appeared not to understand or respond to the most basic instruction. Yet as soon as this volunteer entered the room and during the time he led the group, the students were engaged, capable, and remarkably well behaved.

I was anxious to chat with this gifted volunteer, expecting him to have a day job working with the special needs population. If not, then surely he was the parent of a child with special needs. Well, I was wrong. This volunteer had no training, no background, and no personal tie to anyone with special needs. On weekdays he worked on industrial equipment in a totally unrelated field. He volunteered in this specific role because he sought out the opportunity. He shared that he found great meaning in his service to this class. We only talked briefly that Sunday morning, but the conversation has stayed with me. The volunteer made a point to tell me that it was through this role that he found purpose and personal satisfaction in life. He talked about getting through the weekdays in anticipation of Sundays, energized by his volunteer time with this group of individuals.

Later, the leader of the special needs ministry gave me more background on how this ministry worker found his way to his volunteer role. Originally he was a host during large group in the regular children's ministry. He became acquainted with a few of the individuals with special needs, who were being brought to the large group in order to hear the Bible story. It wasn't long before this guy approached church leaders and asked if they could replace him in his existing host role. He wanted to take the Bible story to the entire class of students with special needs, many of were unable to attend the regular large group story time. The special needs ministry leader, who was also a gifted special education teacher, then provided this new storyteller with a visual board and coaching to better engage these students who all had severe intellectual disability. The volunteer caught on quickly and the rest is history.

As I recount the details of this story I wonder who was serving whom. Just maybe the special needs ministry was serving the volunteer as much as the volunteer was serving the ministry. There is great opportunity whenever a church leader can make a connection between the ministry's needs for help and a church full of prospective volunteers, who need purpose and life meaning. Everyone wins when the "burden" mind-set is abandoned and when the special needs ministry sees itself as a blessing to those who choose to be part of their community.

Tap into teens. Many special needs ministries utilize the service of older students as buddies or class helpers. Some leaders worry that teens are more of a liability, but when teens are trained and set up to win they view their service as an honor and special responsibility. Then their help can become the real arms and legs of the ministry, while also giving the teens an early opportunity *to be the church*. In fact, for many teen volunteers, the experience of working with children with special needs is the primary catalyst for their own spiritual development. While student helpers should always be supervised by screened adult leaders, they add an element of fun that kids with special needs relish. For a teen training outline, see appendix 7.2.

Inclusion Tip: Teen Volunteer Tip

When properly trained, teens can be a valuable asset to a special needs ministry. Develop an application and interview process for prospective young servants, making their selection for service an honor. Provide enlisted teens with a written job description so that they understand the church's expectations for their service. Reward the teens for their assistance by asking a church member to host a summer pool party or game night in their honor.

Get involved in the community. Volunteer or attend an event associated with a local special needs support organization. The Special Olympics or local chapters of various autism education organizations naturally draw interest from people who already have a heart for individuals with special needs. God may bring volunteers to the ministry who weren't already involved in the church. And never doubt God's ability to speak to those volunteers through their service inside the special needs ministry.

Plug in professionals. Special education teachers and pediatric therapists can be great resources to a special needs ministry. Many of these gifted experts relish the idea of contributing their talents to a Kingdom cause. While some professionals may need the weekend to recharge for their weekday job, most are willing to assist the ministry in one way or another. In fact, special education teachers and pediatric therapists appreciate being approached for their input in the ministry. Consider the following ways to invite their contribution:

- Adapt existing curriculum for better special needs engagement.

- Design appropriate craft ideas suitable for participant capabilities.

- Provide Boardmaker® symbols (picture graphics) to match Bible verses and stories.

- Observe the ministry setting and/or specific participants and provide success strategies.

- Recommend equipment and physical aids for special needs environments.

- Help lead volunteer training for special needs caregivers.

- Conduct intake interviews for new ministry participants.

- Advise on current trends in education and legal developments that could affect a church.

Equipping the Volunteers

When a church is in the first stages of building their special needs ministry, there are three particular groups of volunteers that can benefit from special needs specific training:

1. Host team, information desk volunteers, and church greeters who receive first-time guests during weekend programming

2. Special needs buddies and special needs ministry helpers

3. Typical children's ministry workers who will include children with learning differences in their respective environments

To understand why each of these sets of volunteers needs training, let's walk through . . .

The A's of Inclusion

Acceptance: Examine the current culture of the church. Pose the question:

> "If the family of a child with a weakness in social skills, cognitive disability, or physical challenge were to visit our church, would they feel welcome?"

Envision such a family's first visit to the church, starting with their arrival on campus and walking through each step of a Sunday morning experience. Does the host team know how to recognize and appropriately respond to cues indicating a need for special accommodation? How does the children's ministry team react when they first encounter a child who behaves in an unexpected way? Is there a protocol for placing the child in a small group for the first day, or long term? Was person-first language and other disability etiquette used by each church representative? (Be sure to see the disability etiquette pointers in appendix 1.1.) Most importantly, did the various church leaders and volunteers exude warmth and acceptance to the family during each interaction? It is crucial to equip the team of first faces to greet each family with confidence and hospitality.

Dr. Erik Carter, a Professor in the Department of Special Education at Vanderbilt University, has done a tremendous amount of research on the topic of religion and disability. In his book *Including People with Disabilities in Faith Communities*, Dr. Carter describes list of key indicators that give evidence of a welcoming congregation. Below, I have provided Dr. Carter's indicators as well as paraphrased the questions he suggestions churches use to determine how they might become a more inclusive faith community:

Presence: Are individuals with disabilities already present in your programs, in leadership, and on ministry teams?

Accessibility: Does everyone have access to the different locations and facilities in which all programs take place? Are elevators, ramps, and transportation available? Are recreational areas designed so that all children can play together?

Hospitality: Do people inside the congregation engage individuals with disabilities as they would their members without disabilities? Do you see regular interactions such as remembering a name, inviting a person to lunch, celebrating successes, and standing alongside these individuals in difficult times?

A Sense of Shared Lives: Are people with and without disabilities weaved into the common community? Are people with and without disabilities worshipping, fellowshipping, learning, and serving alongside rather than parallel to each other?

Different Motivation: Do we recognize we are missing something vital when individuals with disabilities are not participating? Are we motivated by a clear calling by God to invite individuals with disability to be part of our faith community rather than being motivated by public policy, pity, or pursuit of public praise?

A Recognition of Contributions: Do we seek to discover and unlock the gifts and talents each person possesses? Do we look for the gifts and abilities in people with disabilities?

Proactive Efforts: When we begin planning a new program, event, or building project, do we consider the needs of people who don't yet attend our church or consider additional needs our existing members may have in the future? Do we consider the accessibility of future gatherings and buildings for people with physical disabilities?

Willingness to Learn: Are we open to admitting and learning from our mistakes? Do we ask ourselves and consider how to do something differently? Do we give evidence of a desire to do better?

Reciprocity: Do we help our members with disabilities discover their gifts? Do we equip those same individuals to use those gifts on behalf of others? Are we intentionally looking for and providing ways individuals with disabilities can serve others?[5]

A church host training event may enable the church to answer the above questions. Videotaping and posting the training session online may enable more volunteers to learn from the valuable information shared. (Online training is a great way to equip volunteers who can't attend an important meeting or who are serving as a last-minute sub.)

In appendix 7.3, I have included a fairly descriptive document and my notes from Grace Church's (Greenville, South Carolina) host team training event.

Accommodation: Begin thinking about the most common needs and range of differences the church can expect to encounter as it becomes more special needs friendly. A church might host a brainstorming session with representatives from the children's ministry staff, facilities personnel, church security team, special education experts and selected parents. Invite these participants to dialogue through an average Sunday, midweek, or VBS experience for a child with special needs. Review the variety of activities and environments that may require accommodation adjustments. Consider the following issues:

- Physical barriers to space (e.g., no elevator access, lack of visual or acoustical borders)

- Loud sounds or bright lights

- Activities requiring fine motor skills or gross motor ability

- Learning exercises necessitating independent reading

- Tasks involving teamwork

- Snacks/Allergies

- Transitions from one environment to another, through hallways

- Quantity and quality of planned activities (too few versus too many)

Through the discussion, anticipated challenges can surface and solutions may then be developed before real problems materialize. Also, the desired structure of the ministry may begin to take shape, and the church's policies will naturally emerge, which in turn will determine the issues that need to be covered in a volunteer training event. It is during this time that special education professionals or therapists can address possible behavioral responses from a student experiencing frustration. These same field experts can share their knowledge for how the public schools and other organizations address these issues and develop success strategies. All of these subjects will produce the meat of material to be covered in a training event for special needs buddies and class helpers.

For a list of possible topics to be covered in a special needs ministry handbook and volunteer training event, see appendix 7.1 for ideas for special needs ministry policies and volunteer training topics.

Advancement: Last, begin thinking about how the church can provide opportunities to spur forward the spiritual advancement of students with special needs. A ministry team may never fully grasp their eternal impact in the lives of students with cognitive delays or intellectual disability. However, when learning experiences are planned to engage all of a child's senses and when Bible truths are communicated in tangible ways, children of every learning preference and ability will benefit. And in order for the church to offer such learning opportunities, virtually every volunteer will need inspiration and ideas to make Bible stories come alive. Training sessions on teaching techniques are invaluable to not only the special needs helpers but also all children's ministry volunteers.

8. Behavior and Participant Safety

B ad behavior does not always reflect the state of a child's heart or even sin. In my interviews with education professionals and intervention specialists, they repeatedly said that negative behavior is a means for communication rather than display of character deficiency. Prior to researching the topic of special needs inclusion, my natural inclination as a young parent and regular children's ministry volunteer was to quickly correct a disruptive child, to establish authority, and in some situations, allow the child to experience consequences for their poor choices. But after listening to the stories of so many experts in this area and then implementing their recommended strategies, I have changed my view and how I respond to "misbehavior." By offering a different lens to better understand undesirable behavior, I hope to enable churches to develop a more compassionate and appropriate response. Some behavior challenges will have easier solutions. While other problems will be more complicated, requiring a range of possible options for the participant with special needs and for the church.

Behavior Is Communication

When children are "misbehaving," researchers have found that they are nearly always trying to communicate a need for one of the following:

1. A tangible object

How often have you seen a child cry, scream, or physically act out in an effort to get a desired toy? We aren't surprised when we see this behavior in the toddler room. But the reality is that, sometimes older kids who lack strong communication skills express their frustration similarly.

2. A physical or sensory need

A child may have a physical need or the desire for a certain sensory sensation but not be able to distinguish that need as the source of their discomfort. The best example of this is a two-year-old who skipped an afternoon nap. By 4:00 p.m., that tired toddler is probably in a pretty ornery state and may even be resisting the urge to sleep. Rarely, if ever, would we hear that toddler say, "Mom, my issue is that I need sleep!" The same may be true for a hungry child. The child who needs to eat may not have the self-awareness or communications skills to convey the problem with their growing appetite. Their body tells them they have an unmet need but recognizing and communicating that exact need isn't always natural or possible for some kids.

Along similar lines, many children with special needs have a legitimate physical requirement for sensory input. For some kids that might be exhibited through bursts in energy, like jumping on a trampoline or pulling/pushing a heavy box across the floor. For another child, they receive sensory input through a tight squeeze or by wearing a weighted vest. **When a child's needs fail to be met, undesirable behaviors may surface.** So, it's unfortunate that a kid who is seeking to have his underlying and physical cravings met becomes viewed and labeled as a troublemaker.

> Bad behavior does not always reflect the state of a child's heart or even sin.

3. To escape a demand, an activity, or a sensory stimulation

In any group environment, not every child will enjoy or excel at the same activities. And sometimes an undesirable behavior will surface when a student is instructed to do an exercise that he doesn't like to do or can't do well. For example, a child with a weakness in fine motor skills may not be so great at manipulating scissors, peeling small stickers, or holding crayons. So as you might expect, this same child may not get excited about a craft that requires all those steps. In fact, he might show his displeasure by becoming agitated when encouraged to take a seat at the activity table. He might even run off! As another example, there might be a student who struggles with auditory processing, so they don't look forward to small group time. Without visual aids, story illustrations, or experiential participation, they're enduring a lecture reminiscent of the "WAH wa Wah wa WAH" babble that Charlie Brown tolerated from his infamous school teacher. It should be anything but surprising when such a student becomes restless after a while, if not disruptive.

Along similar lines, a child may encounter a sensory stimulation that is unpleasant or even painful (like fingernails on a chalkboard to some of us). An example of a sensory experience that causes distress could be any of the following:

- Strong smells

- Bright lights

- Loud music or noises

- Humming sounds or vibrations sometimes associated with building noises (A/C, heater)

- High-energy environment

A child's behavior may quickly deteriorate as their need to escape this environment (and its unwanted sensory input) grows. In fact, a behavioral meltdown can oftentimes be tied back to a contributing factor like these examples.

4. To get attention from adults or peers

Any person who has worked among children can attest to the fact that kids act out when they want attention. Whether at school, church, or amidst a child's birthday party, we've all seen kids exhibit clear signs of needing love and attention. For children with or without special needs, the desire to be noticed and included can be a driving force behind undesirable behavior.

Identify the Child's Core Need

For children and students who struggle to behave appropriately, developing a successful accommodation plan largely hinges on identifying the root cause of undesirable behavior. Almost always kids have legitimate needs that warrant attention. Sometimes however, those same kids can't or don't express their needs appropriately. When undesirable behaviors surface in the church setting, the goal of the ministry team is to:

1. Interpret the core need driving the behavior.

2. Solve the problem and work to prevent the problem from occurring again.

3. Work with the student (and their parents, when possible) to develop consistent and appropriate communication for expressing their needs.

With patience, tenacity, and ingenuity, the vast majority of behavior problems can be solved. (See the Special Needs Ministry Policies and Volunteer Training Topics in appendix 7.1 for tips on behavior management.) Occasionally however, some behavior challenges require a more complex approach that may or may not be within the capabilities of the church. So, let's walk through some possible solutions steps.

> Almost always kids have legitimate needs that warrant attention. Sometimes however, those same kids can't or don't express their needs appropriately.

Document Behaviors

Whenever a child exhibits undesirable communication (in other words, undesirable behavior), consider the four possible reasons for bad behavior that we just outlined. Walk through the four common causes of undesirable behavior (tangible object; physical or sensory need; to escape an activity or attention; to gain attention) seeing if any could apply to the situation in question. Perhaps a lightbulb immediately turns on and the link is made between this stimulus and the student's (undesirable) reaction. If you've figured out the puzzle for the particular situation, then you can jump further in this chapter where we talk about the solution path forward. If you are still scratching your head, trying to solve the behavioral riddle, then you may want to consider the following investigative activity: Create an ABC Conduct Log.

Take an 8.5 x 11 sheet of paper, holding it in the landscape position. Fold the paper two times so that there are three columns. Label each column as follows:

A–Antecedent: In this column, note what happened immediately before the inappropriate behavior. Use this column to see if a trend develops. Is there something triggering the behavior? For example, is the child displaying inappropriate behavior at the same time of day? Or perhaps the behavior is surfacing just prior to an activity the student doesn't enjoy. A pattern may surface that indicates the student's medication is wearing off, they're becoming tired, or feeling hungry. Occasionally, you may see that a student acts out when they are working alongside or under the direction of a particular individual.

B–Behavior: Reflect on the details of the problematic incident or exhibited behaviors. Note the child's actions and reactions. Look for what message the child is trying to communicate. For example, did the child want a toy and lacked the language to ask for it? Was the music too loud? Was the child overstimulated?

C–Consequences: Describe what happened immediately after the behavior. Note how group leaders or buddies reacted to the behavior and what consequences were enacted. Are the reactions or consequences of the caregivers unintentionally feeding the inappropriate behavior? Did the undesirable behavior escalate as teachers addressed the situation or enacted consequences for the child?

Pull in the class leaders who may have been present for the behavior problems. As they recall the details of the situation, note their responses in the appropriate columns. As facts are recounted, pieces of the puzzle may begin to come together. For more complex situations, consider inviting the input of an experienced special needs professional. (**Important:** be careful not to share the name(s) of the child or their family in order to protect their privacy.)

After analyzing the incident or trend in incidents, a cause and a solution may start to surface. Solutions may include any of the following:

• A student not previously matched with a one-on-one helper is now assigned a buddy. This helper may assist the student so that tasks become less challenging and more enjoyable. The personal aide may also accompany the student to an alternate ministry setting (e.g., the special needs ministry environment) for short or longer periods of time, in order to offer the child a different activity or a calming environment.

• A student is provided a parent-approved snack at a time when they are becoming hungry.

• A student is incented to participate constructively in a certain environment or activity by working toward a reward.

• A student is encouraged to jump on the trampoline or do heavy exercise when signs of restlessness begin to surface.

• A student is encouraged to take a break in a quiet area or relax on a beanbag as needed.

The list of possible strategies could go on, but please remember that these ideas are helpful for a variety of behavior problems that surface, regardless of a child's ability or disability.

Once a cause or trend is identified, the majority of behavior problems can be prevented. For example, if a child has a meltdown or tantrums every time they are asked to complete a fine motor task, brainstorm about how the child's helpers and teachers can remove obstacles:

> **The more prepared a child's buddy or group leader is for a behavior, the less likely it will occur.**

• Pre-cut craft pieces before the student arrives.

• Offer alternate ways for the student to participate. (Could the child respond verbally rather than in writing?)

• Provide different materials such as chunky finger crayons or adaptive scissors.

The more prepared a child's buddy or group leader is for a behavior, the less likely it will occur.

Parent Involvement

Oftentimes problems can be solved and solutions crafted without the help of parents. This is where discernment and judgment are required. If the ministry staff has a strong relationship with a child's parent and/or parents take an active role in their child's accommodation plan, then parents should be included in conversations regarding behavior and changes to the child's accommodation plan.

Personally speaking, I'd want to know if an ABC log had been created for my child, and if there was ongoing discussion as to how the church should accommodate him/her. However, after oodles of church and parent interviews, I've come to learn that not every parent takes my same approach. For a variety of reasons, some parents do not want honest conversations about their child's needs and behaviors. Some mothers and fathers are not at a place where they can process this type of situation for their child and the surrounding issues. Because a church may fear losing a relationship with the parents if they broach such a delicate topic, ministry leaders may in some cases opt to address the problem and develop the solution without parents' help. Again, this is not ideal. But I have heard enough stories to know that, in some cases, developing a solution without involving the parents is a realistic solution when given the circumstances.

The child's possible special needs are secondary to solving a behavior problem.

When a participant's behaviors pose a threat to anyone's safety, including themselves, other ministry participants, or the volunteers, then the solution path will always involve a conversation with the parents. Always. And we'll discuss the issue of physical safety later in this chapter.

When the parents are pulled into discussions regarding their child's behaviors (hopefully more often than not), ministry leaders should approach the subject with great sensitivity. Dialogue is best initiated with affirmations of the church's love for the child while repeating the desire to see the child succeed in the church setting. Delicate conversations are best in person (never email!) and presented in a non-alarming tone. It often helps if the church leader starts the conversation by mentioning the fact that it is not uncommon for a participating child to require individualized strategies. (And this is true regardless of a child's abilities or disabilities.) When the church leader normalizes the need for parent conversations and participant-specific accommodation plans, parents may grow more comfortable and less defensive. The parent conversation will be more productive if the dialogue is centered on potential solutions and doesn't get stuck on the problems. In fact, the conversation is more likely to go well if the church leader initiates the dialogue with solutions already in mind. In cases where a child is exhibiting problematic behavior and where there are suspected but not disclosed (or diagnosed) special needs, it is wise to avoid mention of any possible disability. The child's possible special needs are secondary to solving a behavior problem, especially if Mom and Dad aren't ready to discuss the situation with church leadership.

Promoting Constructive Communication

To promote constructive communication, a reward system may sometimes be part of the strategy for improving undesirable behavior. For instance, if a child struggles with hitting other children, a buddy or class leader may say, "Jake, you will get a sticker if you raise your hand to tell us you want something rather than hitting a friend." For a period, Jake's buddy may need to keep a sticker or a reward log nearby to note Jake's good choices in a way he can see them and feel a sense of accomplishment right away. After a student has mastered one area of challenge (e.g., raising their hand rather than hitting), the reward or public praise may no longer be needed. Then the buddy or teacher can transition to working on a different communication or behavioral goal.

Understand the Individual

Tonya Langdon, special needs facilitator for Skyline Church in San Diego, California, shares a story that perhaps best illustrates how a church can help a child overcome notable behavior hurdles. (And in the case of this story, it was without the cooperation of parents.)

Several years ago, an elementary-aged student who we will call Emily* reacted strongly to most direction inside the church small group environment. The church was never informed of any special needs for Emily. However, her class helpers repeatedly witnessed behaviors commonly associated with diagnoses under the umbrella of mental health providers. In addition, Emily's home life was anything but a model situation. Challenging behaviors quickly escalated to unacceptable conduct from Emily, consistently wearing down the volunteer team and disrupting the other children's learning experience. Tonya was called in to observe and develop a course of action. "I had a sense that Emily wanted respect and her negative behavior was a way of seeking attention. While she was demanding her needs be met in an unacceptable and unconstructive fashion, the fact remained that she was trying to communicate her desires to her leaders."

Tonya began shadowing Emily, taking responsibility for her during church programming. Tonya was attentive to Emily yet at times she ignored her, giving the child the impression that her independence was allowed and that her negative behavior wasn't worthy of additional attention. Tonya picked her battles and didn't correct Emily for every little disruption (as had happened in the past). While Tonya's approach seemed counterintuitive, giving the appearance of indifference at certain times actually worked in her favor by gaining a more compliant attitude from Emily. It wasn't long before Emily's disruption toned down to the point that remaining in the class was no longer an issue.

The beauty of this story is that, by acknowledging Emily's needs and successfully managing her otherwise undesirable behavior, Emily was enabled to spiritually develop during her time in church programming. After working one-on-one with Emily for several weeks, Tonya discovered the young girl had a fondness for chewing gum. One Sunday morning, Tonya placed a piece of gum on the edge of a table, nonchalantly mentioning it was a reward available to Emily if she successfully participated in the day's Bible instruction. To Tonya's relief, it wasn't long before Emily indicated her desire to attempt the Scripture memory exercise. With devoted assistance, Emily began mastering the weekly assignments. In the meantime, Tonya developed a nonverbal code for communicating with

Emily. "She doesn't self-regulate well. So, she needs visual cues signaling her actions are moving in an unhealthy or disruptive direction," Tonya explains of Emily's inability to control impulses and her need for guidance. Indeed, Emily responded well to the hand gestures Tonya developed for what otherwise would have been an embarrassing public rebuke. Emily's teachers also learned how to help Emily experience success in the church setting. While every staff member and volunteer would agree that working with Emily was sometimes draining, her improvement was worth celebrating. A couple of years later, Emily completed a significant portion of the church-offered education curriculum. Tonya captured the opportunity for positive reinforcement and affirmation, creating a special award for Emily's achievement. Tonya noted: "Because of the home life and background of this child, the award was likely the first-ever positive recognition Emily received. I'm so thankful our church was blessed by the opportunity to provide one of the few experiences of unconditional love in this child's life."

*Name changed for privacy

When Tonya was relaying this story, she reflected on the fact that well-meaning church volunteers often see a child exhibiting perceived behavior problems. An adversarial relationship may develop, especially when those leading or teaching the child lack an understanding for neurological drivers fueling the inappropriate or even defiant behavior. Tonya made a wise point that I have remembered and since implemented when I'm volunteering—when a child's leaders provide them freedom through controlled choices, the dynamics can change, and sometimes dramatically. Tonya wisely summed it all up: "Children with special needs tire of being forced to conform. Already difficult behavior is more likely to intensify when the child is given further reason to rebel. Instead, when we pick our battles carefully, allowing the child to make non-disruptive choices, we often see the individual warm to our volunteers and actually want to engage constructively."

Not surprising after this experience and others, Skyline Wesleyan Church places particular emphasis inside the teacher training for all children's ministry volunteers on the importance of understanding and relating to each child.

Addressing Issues of Physical Safety

When a child's behavior threatens the safety of any ministry participant, including the participant themselves, the church is compelled to act. Ensuring the safety of any child (with or without special needs) and of those around them should be the top priority of the church. In the sections that follow, I will attempt to address some of the more complex behavior challenges churches occasionally wrestle through. While all of the issues brought up here have at one point or another come to my attention from a special needs ministry leader, many of these behaviors and concerns also occur among children without special needs. To prevent the perception or practice of discrimination, it is important that the behavior concerns and consequences be addressed consistently and uniformly among participants with and without disability.

> To prevent the perception or practice of discrimination, behavior concerns should be handled consistently among participants with and without a disability.

Elopement

Many churches with established special needs ministries can share stories about a participant who ran away during church. Those ministry leaders will laugh now about the pursuit that ensued and the happy ending. But they'll also recall their near heart attack when they discovered a student was missing!

Occasionally, parents will disclose their child's propensity to run off, wander, or bolt. Candidly, it is a much easier situation for the church (and ultimately for the student) when parents are forthright about their child's tendencies. But oftentimes, the church ministry team will discover only through experience that a particular participant is prone to elopement. And as you might guess, these "surprises" aren't the kind staff and volunteers enjoy.

The good news is that with appropriate supports, kids who run off can nearly always be successfully included in the church. But their accommodation plan will require additional safety measures. Dennis Debbaudt is a nationally recognized autism safety expert and the consultant behind AutismRiskManagement.com. Dennis worked with me to develop the following guidance to help churches when elopement is a risk factor:

During the intake process, ask parents if the child is known to occasionally wander or run off. Inquire if there is a catalyst to elopement. Is the child trying to escape an activity? Is he/she prone to running off in response to a certain type of situation or a change? If you can gather some clues, a problematic situation could possibly be recognized and prevented by the ministry team. In order for the parents to trust you, convey through your voice tone and body language that the church intends to accept the child, so they will share honestly. With the parents' help, consider completing an "emergency contact form" available online at www.AutismRiskManagement.com.

Eliminate transitions and travel for a child prone to elopement. If a student has in the recent past run off during church (or the parents have informed the church of this possibility), then their accommodation plan should be developed with the goal of preventing elopement. Risk increases with transitions such as moving between rooms. As a result, it is best to eliminate any need for the participant to travel during their church experience. For example, walking down a hall (even to the bathroom) may increase the odds of an elopement situation. For a child who has previously been included in the typical ministry setting and has begun demonstrating the propensity to run away for a period they may need to be removed from the typical ministry environment. Even though the student may otherwise thrive in small groups and large groups among their typical peers, an updated church accommodation plan may be developed so that safety is the primary focus. Very often, such a student is best served inside the special needs class, where more volunteers are added and the room features a floor plan designed with elopement prevention in mind.

Provide a confined and secure environment for participants prone to running off. Designate a learning environment that has at least two sets of doors (and ideally, three) between the inside of the class and outside the building. For example, the child might be placed in a learning environment inside a special needs ministry suite. So, when the family arrives at church, they would enter through exterior doors, walk through a hall or open area before entering a second set of lockable doors and into a suite. Once inside the suite, the child would then go through another door or half-door to their classroom. For a child to leave the building, they would have to escape three sets of doors. If fire code requires direct access to the outside, then discuss safety options with your building inspector and fire marshal. Undoubtedly, fire alarms would be installed on such doors.

Inside the secure environment, provide a handicap accessible bathroom. If this isn't possible, and the bathroom requires travel away from the secure area, a plan should be developed for trips to the bathroom. Decide who will accompany the individual to the bathroom or anywhere else on campus.

Install a door alarm on classroom doors. When the alarm switch is turned on and the door is opened, the sound goes off. The sound may prompt class leaders to respond to a student's attempt to elope.

Train the security team and church greeters to recognize potential bolters. A church may want to post security at key spots outside buildings as well. For high-risk situations, security may be advised when a particular student arrives on campus so as to be available and nearby in case help is needed. However, be sure to avoid over- or under-reaction.

Develop an elopement response plan. Involve the church's security team, facilities personnel, and special needs ministry volunteers in this plan. Who should be notified first? Who will make a decision about a potential lockdown? How will the lockdown be initiated? What means of communication will be used (e.g., pager, cell phone, walkie-talkie, etc.)? Who will place the 911 call on behalf of the church? Identify all nearby water sources and other hazardous locations in close proximity to the church building (e.g., busy intersection). Consider establishing a code word for an active elopement situation when using public means of communication. Train the team for appropriate communications while pursuing the student, keeping verbal communications simple, nuance free, and to avoiding use of slang, jokes, and figures of speech.

> If a certain behavior is deemed so inappropriate that a child cannot remain in school, then the same should be true for the church. And oftentimes, it is wise for a church to establish a lower threshold for expulsion than the school.

Invite local law enforcement to be part of the response plan. With parents' permission, provide key information to police in advance. When law enforcement officers know how to appropriately respond, especially with the nuances of a particular individual in mind, the odds of a happy ending increase dramatically.

Monitor and modify the accommodation plan for identified students. Many individuals will outgrow their tendencies or learn new skills, reducing their risk of elopement. Work with parents to remind and reinforce better communication choices, helping a child find safer ways to relay their needs and desires. Over time, the need for increased safety measures may diminish. Take small steps to see if the student can reengage in less secure, typical ministry settings.

Aggressive Behavior

In cases where a child is exhibiting aggressive behavior or behavior that jeopardizes the safety of anyone (including the child themselves), it is important that the church walk through the steps already outlined in this chapter to identify and solve the problem. Nearly always, strategies can be implemented that enable a child to remain in the church's care. However, in some situations, the church may not be equipped to serve a child whose behavior is physically threatening.

In the public school system, each school or school district develops, adopts, and implements a code of student conduct. The purpose of the code of student conduct is to establish standards, policies, and procedures related to student behavior at school.[1] And the ultimate goal behind the code and its policies is to ensure that a school environment "foster[s] the health, safety and social and emotional well-being of students."[2] As part of the school's policies, provisions are outlined for consequences to behaviors jeopardizing the safety of the school environment, including suspensions or expulsions.

Along the same lines, the Americans with Disabilities Act permits childcare centers to exclude children with disabilities from their programs if their presence would pose a *direct threat* to the health or safety of others.[3]

The church can take valuable queues from the public school system and the ADA laws. If a child is exhibiting behavior that would result in notable disciplinary action inside the school system, including suspension or expulsion from school, then a church is wise to adopt similar consequences. One of the primary reasons a child might be suspended or expelled from the school setting is so that the school can ensure the safety of the other students. If a certain behavior is deemed so inappropriate that a child cannot remain in school, then the same should be true for the church. And oftentimes, it is wise for a church to establish a lower threshold for expulsion than the school. This is because unlike schools, churches are not provided the funding (tax dollars) and resources (extensive training) to accommodate the most challenging behavior situations. If a child has shown aggressive behaviors and can be accommodated in the public school setting only as long as they have a personal aid and are placed inside a room with enhanced security features, then a certain church may or may not have the appropriate resources to safely accommodate the same child in their ministry environment.

A church reserves the right to accommodate a child in the way that ensures everyone's safety and in accordance with the recommendations of its insurance provider. A church can require a child and a family to abide by certain arrangements for individualized accommodation. And if the parents and/or the participant with special needs do not agree to follow those arrangements, the church may graciously decline accommodation. At that time, the church leader may offer genuine blessing on the family to pursue another church home that better fits their needs. It is so important that in a delicate and difficult conversation like this, the church leader conveys genuine care for the family. It is also important that the church leader keep the door open for their return.

I am familiar with churches that have gone through similar situations, eventually to have the family return after unsuccessful attempts to find another church. Although it can be through a painful process, a family eventually comes to terms with the type of accommodation their child requires in order to ensure his safety and the safety of others.

It is important that the analysis and measures described throughout this chapter are utilized. The purpose of this chapter is to offer strategies for providing accommodation, even in challenging situations. Turning away a child because you can't accommodate them is a last resort.

Small Churches

Every church does not have the same resources. As a result, not every church will have the ability to safely meet every accommodation need. Each of the following factors may impact the type of accommodation the church can safely provide:

- Funds to contract a trained and bonded nurse (e.g., provide medical care, dispense medication, or diapering)

- Availability of physical space

- Facilities with an appropriate floor plan and enhanced security features (e.g., to prevent elopement)

- Active presence of a church security team

- Skill-set and aptitude of the ministry volunteers (e.g., some caregivers are naturally gifted and/or trained to work with especially complex behavior situations)

I want to note here that none of these reasons should be viewed as a loophole justification or excuse for avoiding the extra steps sometimes required to include a child with special needs. Instead, I hope these are helpful guide points to smaller churches that may be working to determine (and feel unnecessarily guilty for) their limitations. I have been truly amazed and touched by the number of small congregations who have reached out to me the last few years seeking help and guidance as they worked fervently to welcome families with some of the most complex special needs.

Before we leave this topic, I want to bring up some key wording in the ADA laws that may provide guidance to churches and especially small churches. Most childcare centers in the United States are required by law to comply with the Americans with Disabilities Act or ADA. The exception to the law's coverage is childcare centers that are actually run by religious entities such as churches, mosques, or synagogues, which are exempt from compliance to title III of the ADA. So, while the regulations exempt childcare provided in the church setting from ADA compliance, there is guidance that can translate well to churches. The law requires that covered childcare centers make *reasonable modifications* to their policies and practices to integrate children, parents, and guardians with disabilities into their programs *unless doing so would constitute a "fundamental alteration" of the program.* The law also requires that these same centers must provide appropriate auxiliary aids and services needed for effective communication with children or adults with disabilities, *when doing so would not constitute an "undue burden."*[4] From the wording, we see how the U.S. government recognizes the potential resource limitations of a childcare provider when matched with the level of some person's specific needs. It is reasonable to deduce that not every childcare provider can provide the aids and services necessary for every individual with disabilities. I think there is a correlation to churches. The church led by a bi-vocational pastor and a volunteer staff is going to reach the level of "fundamental alteration of the program" and "undue burden" more quickly than the megachurch that employs a multilayered staff with state-of-the-art facilities. The point I want to make is that not every church can safely accommodate a child with higher associated risks. And we should be careful not to embarrass or publicly shame a church that wisely recognizes its accommodation limitations.

Automatic Removal of a Student

According to the IDEA (Individuals with Disabilities Education Act), a school system may remove a student without regard to whether the behavior is determined to be a manifestation of a child's disability, if the child:

- Carries or is in possession of a weapon to school

- Knowingly possesses or uses illegal drugs, or solicits the sale of a controlled substance

- Has inflicted serious bodily injury upon another person while at school.[5]

Churches are wise to mirror the response of schools, immediately removing a child when any of the above factors is present. In fact, church leaders may find it necessary to call 911 immediately upon discovering any of the above situations or occurrences.

Final Words

I know that some of the material in this chapter can be hard to wrestle with and think through. But my hope is that the material presented here, along with the rest of the book, will help church leaders and volunteers have more effective conversations about some of the more complicated, even legal matters, associated with special needs ministries in a church setting. I write this section taking into account all my different related roles and experiences: as a writer and researcher, as a church consultant, as a ministry volunteer and as a mom with a child in church environments every week.

It has to be said: if a child or student's behavior poses a threat to their own safety or any other participant in the ministry, then the church's accommodation of the child needs to be thoroughly and prayerfully examined. Well-thought-out boundaries should be carefully designed to protect the church and the people it serves, so they can continue to point people to Jesus.

In the most extreme situations, the church should do its best to minister to the family outside the confines of childcare. In some cases, the church might offer to contribute funds to the family to help with childcare. Perhaps parents can secure the services of a specially trained caregiver who can supervise and aid the child inside the family's home. A children's ministry or special needs ministry leader might also provide materials from small group lessons, helping parents further the spiritual growth of their child at home. Another way a church can continue or grow their relationship with the family is by assigning them a mentor from the church's care team. It is important that the church think outside the box, actively pursuing a relationship with the family, just as Jesus Christ pursues a relationship with each of us.

> It is important that the church think outside the box, actively pursuing a relationship with the family, just as Jesus Christ pursues a relationship with each of us.

9. FAQs (Frequently Asked Questions)

In this section, I want to address any lingering questions on other topics that haven't been addressed yet in the book. The two subjects I receive the most questions about are behavior management and curriculum modification. Chapter 8 was written to offer a fairly thorough response to some of the more common and complex behavior-related questions. And in this book, we do not address curriculum modification extensively.

FAQ: What if the parents and student ministry leaders disagree on placement of a teen with special needs?

MY ANSWER: A good rule of thumb is for the church to mirror the student's accommodation at school. So the first step to figuring out how to make things work at church is to find out how the child participates and learns at school. The following paragraph is a good example of a way to begin a conversation with parents and explain what information would be helpful:

"As a church, our goal is to work alongside a child's parents and together, help the student develop spiritually. And we know that every child is unique. So, oftentimes we need to learn more about individual participants in our ministry in order to connect with them in a positive and meaningful way. We can have a better relationship with your son or daughter when we understand how your child experiences success at school. For example, if a student receives some form of assistance at school or learns in a specialized setting for part of their school day, it's smart for us to think about if similar supports are needed or available here at church. We may or may not be able to assist a student in every way that would be ideal, but we've got to ask the questions. This knowledge helps the leaders serving your child, the peers interacting with him, and perhaps most benefits your child. Since we are partnering with you in your child's spiritual growth journey, we'd love for you to share more about how your child learns and interacts at school."

Possible questions to ask parents:

- Does your child spend *all*, *some*, or *none* of the school day in a setting among typical peers?

- During what subject(s) or time(s) of the day does your child receive special assistance or differentiated instruction?

- Does your child receive individualized attention to help him through routine classwork?

- Are lessons, instruction, or tests or modified around his or her abilities?

- Is your child accustomed to participating in group discussions with typical peers at school?

- What behavior supports does your child have at school (sticker chart, behavior plan)?

It is important for the person talking with the family to recognize that the parents are the number one part of the child's support team. Hearing them and acknowledging their goals for their child is nearly always crucial for getting on the same page or diffusing any tension.

If the church leader discovers in the course of this conversation that the student receives a notable amount of special instruction, individualized attention, or altered instruction/testing at school, then the leader's goal is to help the parents compare those needs and supports with their expectations for their child at church. Sometimes as parents process the situation aloud, they begin to understand the concerns that prompted the conversation to begin with. And an agreed upon solution is not hard to find. Other times, parents don't see the gap in where things are at school and where they are at church. And in these cases the church leader might ask parents to give their student and the ministry team a 3–4 week trial doing something different. That something different might take the form of an assigned peer-helper or adult aid. Or it may mean that the student with special needs participates in an alternate activity during some or all small group discussion times. And it can be a combination of any of the above and change on a weekly basis. One week's small group discussion may be on a topic that the student can and should fully participate in. And the next week the subject matter may be sensitive and on a topic beyond the student's intellectual or emotional capabilities.

Keep in mind that it is not the responsibility of a church leader to make all the people happy all of the time. It is their responsibility to set everyone up for success: the individual with special needs, their peers, and the leaders serving them all.

FAQ: What about parent support groups?

Our church recently announced intentions to launch a special needs ministry. Parents are especially eager to start a parent support group as part of the new ministry.

MY ANSWER: Special needs ministry really is ministry to an entire family. So, as the church builds its special needs ministry, creating venues to encourage parents and foster their spiritual growth is crucial. However, I personally advise churches to focus *first* on developing successful accommodation for the child. And there are several reasons I prioritize the child over the parent in the initial stages of ministry:

1. If we can't successfully care for the child, the lack of childcare will be a barrier to parent participation in those support groups. This is especially true for single parents.

2. The church already offers ministry environments for adults. If a church can successfully care for a child with special needs, then the

parents are enabled to attend the worship services and small groups already offered. While those venues may not speak to the unique life circumstances of special needs, they do provide opportunities for those parents to grow spiritually.

3. Coordinating and facilitating parent support groups *well* requires an investment of time and a leader gifted in offering pastoral care.

Let me explain the third point a little further. One of my early experiences researching on this topic was attending a church-hosted mother's support group. Reflecting on that night, I remember many women in the room who were at different places emotionally and spiritually. Their stories revealed vulnerability and raw emotions. And the views and opinions expressed were sometimes appreciated by the others, but at other times were received as offensive or insulting. After the meeting when I was alone with the group's facilitator, I inquired about the group dialogue. I was curious to know if some mothers left with hurt feelings. This wise leader then explained that support groups require an investment of time both before and after a meeting. Prior to that night's gathering, this leader had met one-on-one with most of the attending moms. She knew their stories and was in-tune with where they were emotionally and spiritually. And to help keep the conversation healthy, she had coached several attending mothers to interject as needed, helping to guide the group dialogue. Along the same lines, phone calls and coffee times were likely to be scheduled in the coming week. She and some of the other ministry-minded moms would follow up with those group participants who were in especially rough places or maybe needed a "repair" conversation after the group gathering.

This example shows just how much intentionality, time, and follow-up can be required. And in the early days, the ministry may not be poised to host a special needs support group. In addition, for the group times to be worthwhile, it requires a strong (and spiritually mature) facilitator to guide those gatherings. This group facilitator may or may not be the same person coordinating the day-to-day aspects of the special needs ministry because a different gift set is required to lead a parent support group. Often, after the special needs ministry has been running for a while, the church is better able to identify spiritually mature parents who can also help anchor the dialogue inside the parent support group gatherings.

Katie Garvert, a seasoned special needs ministry leader, reflects on her experience when she was shaping a budding special needs ministry for Woodmen Valley Chapel (Colorado Springs, Colorado):

> Several years ago when I started as Access Ministry's coordinator, people were excited to see the church taking steps to build a special needs ministry. While our church was still brainstorming a bit, families were anxious to see us start a parent support group. Without a doubt, I felt like that would be an important part of our ministry offering. But I surprised a few people when I said we needed one or two years before we tackled the parent piece of ministry. In the beginning, I concentrated on creating ministry environments for individuals with special needs (children, students, and adults) as well as equipping their volunteer leaders.
>
> Two years later, as promised, we launched a parent support group. Around the same time we began offering quarterly respite events. Now, I'm really proud of how our church ministers to the whole family. But I'm also thankful for the time in the beginning when we narrowed our focus. We didn't bite off more than we could chew. Little success after little success, we developed best practices and a strong volunteer base. And so by the time we started parent support groups and respite, we knew what we were doing. And the Access leaders weren't overwhelmed or tired from doing too much at once. Instead, we were all ready and excited to take our ministry to the next level.

FAQ: What about respite care or respite events?

Our church has been approached by parents (or other outside organizations) to consider hosting regular respite nights as a way to jump-start our special needs ministry.

MY ANSWER: Respite is one of the very best ways for a church to meet the physical needs of a family of a child with special needs. However, for a church in the beginning stages of developing a special needs ministry, I would prioritize developing Sunday morning (or weekend services) accommodation and inclusion over respite. Here's why: Planning, staffing and coordinating a respite event can be a big undertaking. And those efforts may sometimes interfere with planning, staffing, and coordinating the Sunday morning aspects of a new special needs ministry. If a parent is able to drop off their child on a Friday night for respite but unable to leave their child on Sunday morning, has the church really done its job?

I found an example of this several years ago when I was first looking for churches to interview that have special needs ministries; someone recommended that I contact a certain church. I heard about the strong reputation the church had built in the community because of weekend respite events for children with special needs. Parents from all over that local area benefited from the church's willingness to provide focused special needs childcare on one Saturday each month. Excited to learn more, I contacted the church asking to talk to someone about the special needs ministry. Sometime later, I received an email from the church staff explaining that the church didn't have a special needs ministry. I was then provided contact information for a person not on staff who ran the respite events. After a little more investigation, I learned that few if any of the families receiving respite attend that particular church. And through some additional conversation, I gathered that the church was not prepared to receive children with special needs on Sundays.

There is absolutely no doubt in my mind that the church was doing a great service and ministry by offering respite. But part of me wished that the same energy devoted toward respite could be directed toward Sunday mornings . . .

- Where children with unique needs could learn about Jesus;

- Where parents could attend small groups and worship services because their children with special needs were receiving safe and loving care;

- Where an entire community of believers could interact, minister to, and learn from the family of a child with special needs.

Respite is a really great way for a church to build a relationship with a family. And to parents desperate for a break to tend to their own needs, few means of ministry are more effective. My hope is that a church would use respite as part of a bigger picture strategy to reach a family and bring them into the body of Christ. In my view, the ultimate goal for a special needs ministry is to bring families into a growing relationship with Jesus Christ. And in order for that to happen, a church has to be prepared to successfully accommodate the child with special needs during regular church programming. **If a mom can leave her child at a Friday night respite event but she can't attend worship on Sunday, then have we fulfilled our mission?**

There are other benefits to making respite a secondary goal of a special needs ministry. By focusing first on accommodating children and teens during regular church programming, the church has the opportunity to learn the "ropes" when there's a naturally lower risk and shorter time frame since it's based around a worship service. In addition, parents are onsite and available for questions or emergencies during church programming and they aren't during respite care. Other issues to consider include budget and risk management. After consulting the church's insurance provider, a church may wisely contract a skilled medical provider to stay onsite while parents are away. In addition to tending to any medical emergencies, this professional may need to dispense medication and provide diapering services, which many churches do not do during regular church programming.

> My hope is that a church would use respite as part of a bigger picture strategy to reach a family and bring them into the body of Christ.

A significant benefit to hosting respite events is that churches can attract additional volunteers to serve regularly in the special needs ministry. While respite was not the focus of my research, repeatedly in conversations, church leaders shared of how the events worked to build community among the volunteers and the families. And respite events provide good, one-time service opportunities for adult small groups and other prospective volunteers who may want to help one time before committing to a regular Sunday rotation within the special needs ministry. I have also heard stories where a person outside the church with an interest in special needs was invited to serve at a respite event. Their experience proved to be meaningful and led them to get more involved in the church and/or the ministry.

For any church considering expanding their ministry into respite, I would encourage them to research organizations offering assistance to churches in this specific area. Because respite is becoming a popular strategy for outreach and ministry, a number of parachurch ministries and consultants have emerged that can provide valuable assistance.

FAQ: How can we publicize our church's new special needs ministry?

We can't wait to get our special needs ministry off the ground! We want people inside and outside our church to know about our new ministry.

MY ANSWER: In the early days of the ministry, I would focus only on publicizing the ministry internally to the church. It takes a little while for the ministry to recruit and train the volunteers and learn through some trial and error. I would encourage a church to serve those attending or attempting to attend before working hard to attract new people. Know that your ministry is meaningful whether it's serving two children or five students with special needs for the first year. When volunteers are coordinating and leading the ministry, it's especially important that their workload is kept at a reasonable pace so they don't feel too stretched or get burnt out quickly. Give the ministry room to grow organically.

Especially in cases where the church proudly gives the ministry visibility, word will spread. I promise. After a church has created a paid staff position for a ministry leader and after that leader has had the opportunity to develop a rhythm, then the ministry may begin to think about intentional outreach in the surrounding community.

FAQ: Who has ownership of the special needs ministry?

Shouldn't the special needs ministry be a ministry of its own, outside the children's ministry?

MY ANSWER: Every church has its own culture and staff strengths. So, determining staff ownership for the special needs ministry is often organization-specific. However, when it comes to successfully including a child with special needs, some level of ownership from the children's ministry team is nearly always required. Similarly, successfully including a middle school or high school aged student would be dependent on ownership inside those respective ministries. If the *"not my area of responsibility"* mentality creeps into the mind-set of any single staff member or lay leader, efforts to include individuals with disability may take some unnecessary detours or stall out.

> A few years ago, I heard the story of a young mother who dropped out of her midweek women's Bible study. This mother's preschool-aged daughter was diagnosed with a mild, high functioning form of autism. While the mother attended Bible study, her little girl was cared for inside the church nursery. During the year, the child began exhibiting some mild behavior challenges associated with sensory needs and overstimulation. Everyone agreed that an additional childcare worker could benefit an already understaffed nursery and provide devoted attention as needed to the child with special needs. Unfortunately, a standoff emerged between the children's ministry and women's ministry directors over whose budget would cover the added childcare worker's expense. The unwillingness of either staff member to give in eventually caused a frustrated and embarrassed young mother to quit attending her church altogether. This situation had an unfortunate and avoidable outcome.

I have become aware of a couple of instances where a children's ministry team sought to place complete ownership for the special needs ministry outside their responsibilities and under the umbrella of another church ministry. There is good logic to involving other ministries in the special needs ministry (such as the church care team or pastoral care leaders). But in almost every case, a partnership of people working together to address a need can have a greater impact than any one person or even two groups working separately and alone.

> Briarwood Presbyterian Church of Birmingham, Alabama, provides a great example of a collaborative staff effort to effectively serve children with special needs. When the demand for special needs buddies exploded a few years ago, the pastor to high school students quickly agreed to allow thirty-six students to serve in a once-a-month buddy rotation for the special needs ministry. This church leader could have fought against the idea of regularly losing his most trusted and active program participants. But instead,

he recognized an opportunity for the youth to get a chance to be the church and not just go to church. Ultimately, the students serving in the special needs ministry would be impacted personally, growing spiritually because of their service. The partnership between three church ministries turned out to be a "win" for everyone involved.

FAQ: What about therapy dogs?

We have a child who is requesting to bring a therapy dog with them while they participate in church. Do you have any guidance on this subject?

MY ANSWER: Service dogs can be beneficial in several ways, such as helping an individual with a physical disability, alerting caregivers of an impending seizure, or warning if a child is about to touch or eat something with a toxic allergen.

To ensure the safety of everyone though, the church may want to require proof of insurance and accreditation for the service dog before permitting the animal in the church. A true service dog has passed rigorous testing and training through an accredited agency that carries the liability policy on the animal. Any dog that has passed those tests is going to pose less risk to other children and adults.

Permitting a home pet in the church environment is not advisable. An example of a reputable organization that requires training and issues insurance is Therapy Dogs International (http://www.TDI-Dog.org).

FAQ: What about class ratios?

What ratio should we try to meet when we staff for better special needs inclusion?

MY ANSWER: It depends.

If a church is primarily using buddies for their special needs ministry, then it's naturally set up for a 1:1 student-to-teacher ratio.* However, keep in mind that if a teen is serving as a buddy, then the teen is not considered the same as a screened and trained adult. With or without special needs, kids should always be in the presence of two screened and trained adult caregivers who are also unmarried. Married adults may serve together, but for the purposes of meeting the two-person rule, the married couple counts only as a single adult. For more on this policy, see the Special Needs Ministry Policies and Volunteer Training Topics in appendix 7.1.

Note: When a buddy is assigned to work with a child with special needs in a ministry environment or class, that buddy should not count toward the overall student-to-teacher ratio in the room. Serving the student with special needs (and not the needs of other room participants) is the top priority and focus of the assigned buddy.

If a church offers a self-contained special needs setting, the ratio is best determined by the specific needs of the participants. And this is why the intake conversations can be so important. As the church interviewer asks parents about their child's abilities and accommodation needs, they should be thinking through staffing requirements.

> One church leader shared that a mother, who was probably nervous that the church would turn their family away, shared minimal information during the intake interview. The parent often said things like "he'll be just fine," and "he doesn't need much help," as she answered the church leader's questions. But before the interview was over, the church leader asked the mother about the environment the child participated in at school. The interviewing leader learned that the student had a one-on-one aide assigned to him all day at school. Taking a cue from this significant piece of information, the church leader added an additional class helper to the special needs ministry environment before the following Sunday. And as a matter of fact, the added class volunteer was a lifesaver! The ministry team then noted that adding a class helper whenever this participant was expected would be a key part of facilitating that child's success.

Sometimes a 1:1 child-to-teacher ratio isn't necessary. As ministry participants learn the routine, becoming familiar with their leaders and their peers, they may require less individualized attention. As a general rule, 3:1 and 4:1 student-to-teacher ratios are good starting places for a special needs ministry environment, assuming there are no significant safety risks. As the needs and risks increase (and to some degree that is to be expected for a special needs ministry setting), the ratio would need to move more toward 2:1

and 1:1 student-to-teacher ratios. With time, ministry leaders will become familiar with the individual needs of the students and can staff church environments appropriately.

FAQ: How should we group participants and handle age separation?

We know it isn't wise to have five-year-olds and nineteen-year-olds participating in the same ministry environment. Can you give guidance on how to group our special needs ministry environments?

MY ANSWER Typically developing five-year-olds and nineteen-year-olds have different life experiences and different areas of interest. The same is true of five-year-olds and nineteen-year-olds with special needs. It is *not* appropriate to accommodate a wide range of ages in the same ministry environment. And this separation becomes even more important as participants approach and go through hormone changes.

Dividing participants according to the preschool, children's ministry (K–5), middle school, and high school age groups works well for typically developing children as well as individuals with special needs. Several churches have thriving ministry environments with modified activities designed for "tweens" with special needs (arbitrary, usually in the 9–14 range), as well as teens with special needs. The Bible lesson and the exercises offered in these settings are designed to be appropriate for the stage of development and physical age of the group participants. The ministry may promote or "graduate" participants from one age group to another using judgment. A good rule of thumb is placing a child in the same age group as they participate in at school.

FAQ: What supplies do we need for the special needs environment?

We want to set up a special needs ministry environment for kids who need an individualized setting during church participation. Any ideas for supplies or furniture for the room? (Our church has a limited budget!)

MY ANSWER While having special equipment for a special needs environment is fantastic, it isn't necessary to have a sensory room or "multi-sensory environment" (MSE) for a church's special needs ministry. Just having a space that the special needs ministry can claim as their own is a great start!

Some of my favorite supplies aren't expensive at all and can be requested as donations from church members. Several churches post a "ministry wish list" on the church website or through the ministry's social media accounts. Oftentimes, church members who can't serve regularly in the special needs ministry are happy to contribute requested items. One of my favorite online sources is www.SpecialNeedsToys.com. TFH USA (the parent company to this website) tests their products to ensure their safety. The company's website and paper catalog provide an endless number of products with varying costs that could be used inside a church's special needs environment. I highly recommend getting a copy of their in-print catalog just to get you thinking and dreaming of what could be. It's a wonderful go-to resource. Here are a few things I'd prioritize adding to your space:

Sound-eliminator headphones: An inexpensive pair of noise reduction ear headphones can help a child who is overwhelmed by the noise of a large group environment.

Mini trampoline with a handlebar: A few jumps on a small trampoline may meet a child's sensory need for exertion while helping them recollect. Be sure to provide a trampoline with a handle for safety.

Timers: Any type of timer that gives a visual representation of time can be helpful to a student who needs preparation for upcoming transitions. Sand timers are an excellent tool that counts down to the next activity without being loud. Students may appreciate carrying a timer with them through Sunday, Wednesday night, or VBS activities with instructions such as, "This activity will last for two turns of the timer." Timers with a five- or ten-minute range are ideal. For older kids, consider providing a stopwatch for them or for their buddy to program, use, and carry throughout their time together.

Small cause-and-effect toys: Offering a fascinating toy (such as a light-up spin wand) to a would-be "runner" may intrigue the child long enough to get from point A to point B without bolting or wandering off. Walking ropes or guide ropes with built-in loops for holding can also give physical guidance to the child who needs concrete direction and is at risk of elopement.

Fidget toys: Keeping a handful of sensory or squeeze toys on hand can help calm, redirect, and fascinate a child who may otherwise be anxious, bored, or disruptive. The website OfficePlayground.com offers a wide variety of stress balls and sensory toys.

Musical instruments: A simple, handheld instrument, such as a tambourine, may provide interest and engage children of all ability levels. In addition, a musical instrument may serve as a cue for upcoming transitions (e.g., chiming a triangle may signal that it is time for children to wrap up a craft and prepare for the Bible story).

Digital music devices: Many children who struggle to learn through traditional means can enjoy and engage in music. Selecting simple songs that reinforce the Bible story or memory verse may be the primary way some students engage in the day's lesson. Play songs with an easily followed melody and repeat the same song(s) several weeks in a row. In addition, playing soothing music may be a good way to create a calming environment for some students.

Pop-up tent: Setting up a simple tent in one corner of the room can designate a certain area of the room as a resting space. Children who need to retreat from the natural chaos of a ministry environment may benefit from a few minutes inside a partially enclosed tent and away from visual distraction. (However, be sure the students are visible to teachers at all times. There should be no place in the room where students can hide from appropriate supervision.)

Beanbag chair: A child who is over-stimulated or agitated may recollect after a few minutes perched in a comfy spot.

Painter's tape: Many children will benefit from visual boundaries and indicators. For example, when we instruct kids to go line up, it may be helpful to have a long strip of painter's tape on the floor marking the line where kids are to stand. Painter's tape can also be used to create visual boundaries on an activity table so that a child can see where his personal space ends and begins. This can be particularly helpful for the student who eats some of his neighbor's snacks or grabs another child's craft pieces while working at the activity table.

Blue and yellow see-through plastic folders: Text on white paper may be hard for some students to read. Placing activity sheets behind a colored overlay may reduce visual stress and help a student follow along when reading is required or activity sheets are utilized.

Reader highlight ruler (blue ruler that highlights words): Providing colored reader rulers can help a struggling reader track the words inside a Bible. When needed, a class helper or buddy may assist the individual by placing the ruler directly on the referenced Scripture. While many pastel colors are effective, a blue overlay is considered to be the most helpful.

Finger crayons or dot markers: These craft tools are ideal for children who have weaker fine motor skills and may provide a more enjoyable experience at the craft table.

FAQ: What is the story behind the pinwheel on the cover?

MY ANSWER: The pinwheel is a concrete illustration for the abstract nature of faith.

All kids learn best when concrete illustrations are offered to explain abstract concepts. And this is especially true for the child with learning differences. In fact, a common attribute of autism is the need for a concrete learning experience in order to process new information. When I first started researching on special needs inclusion in the church setting, I began thinking about ways to teach Bible concepts to kids who were literal learners. One of the first illustrations I developed for teaching in my own church was the use of a pinwheel to explain the concept of faith.

No one has ever **seen** the wind. We've only experienced the effects and results of the wind. And
none of us have ever **seen** God. Just like the movement of a pinwheel makes us **sure** that the wind
exists, we have ways to be **sure** that God exists.
(e.g., answered prayer, the beauty of nature, etc.).

I first used this illustration a few years ago in a VBS setting where we had
a Bible lesson on faith. The children all took turns blowing on a pinwheel
while we talked about how the pinwheel gives us proof that the wind exists.
And we then talked about ways that we could be sure of God's existence
even though we couldn't see Him. That day every child made a pinwheel
craft to take home to remind them that God exists just like the wind exists.

"Now faith is being *sure* of what we hope for and certain of what
we *do not see*." (Hebrews 11:1 NIV)

10. Including Teens with Special Needs

As churches consider how they can better include children with special needs, it's a natural progression to expand the conversation to encompass teens with special needs. After all, our children with special needs grow up to be teens and adults with learning differences and unique needs. We won't specifically address strategies for including adult inclusion here. And admittedly, what we offer throughout the book and in this chapter is limited related to teen inclusion.

The teenage years bring about unique challenges for every child, and those with special needs are no different. The middle school and high school age span is nearly always significant in a person's spiritual development. This is true for those of us with and without identified disabilities.

Part one of this chapter is from an article I wrote in partnership with Fuller Youth Institute. The piece ran in FYI's September 15, 2014 E-Journal and is reprinted in its entirety here. The article provides a story that I suspect represents a common scenario and possible solutions for many student ministry settings. I have left the questions that FYI's journal posted at the end of the article because they are great tools for self-reflection or conversation starters used to dialogue with leaders inside your ministry.

The second part of this chapter is pulled from a series of posts on my blog where I interviewed Katie Garvert. At the time of the interview, Katie led her church's special needs ministry in Colorado Springs, Colorado. A more complete bio of Katie is featured earlier in this book's acknowledgments. Under Katie's leadership and in collaboration with others on the church's staff, her adopted successful approach for transitioning a growing number of children with special needs into the church's student ministry. I think many ministry leaders serving teens can benefit from the best practices Katie shares for helping students with special needs connect inside the church while developing a faith of their own.

Part One: From Fuller Youth Institute's E-Journal, "Refusing to Ignore Teenagers with Special Needs"

Meet John

Every kid has special needs. But John's quirks were a little different than his church leaders were accustomed to. As John aged out of children's ministry and into his teens, his leaders worried about how they could weave him into the student ministry, in particular how he'd fit in a small group.

John's nearly constant desire to recount stats from his beloved sports team wavered between fascinating and irritating. And when John wasn't giving a play-by-play of a recent game, it was hard to follow his train of thought, creating labored interactions for his peers. So they tended to avoid him most of the time.

Other times he became an easy target for jokes.

His youth ministry leaders tried to connect with John, but struggled to read him emotionally. It wasn't uncommon for John to show visible signs of frustration or anxiety whenever there was a schedule change or new visitor. Yet when discussion turned to a sensitive or emotional subject matter, John seemed lost or distracted. This "disconnect" could create awkward moments for his small group. More than once, John blurted out a random sports fact, interrupting the group dynamic at an inopportune time. And his interjections could come off as disrespectful, especially if they happened on the heels of a peer's vulnerable prayer request.

Admirably, John's parents were committed to his regular church attendance. However, **John's youth leaders silently wondered how they could**

include John in the student ministry environment without compromising the other students' church experience.

John lives daily with a diagnosis of autism. And if he's not already in your youth group, he will be soon.

The Rising Rates of Teenagers with Disabilities

More kids like John are becoming part of church youth groups everywhere. The American Academy of Pediatrics reports a 16 percent increase in the prevalence of childhood disability between 2001 and 2011.[1] While the number of kids with physical disabilities decreased (notably), the diagnoses of mental health and neurodevelopmental conditions jumped a whopping 21 percent for this same population. We know from other studies that these changes are largely attributable to the escalating rise in autism specifically. It is currently estimated that 1 in 68 children has been identified with autism spectrum disorder (ASD), **a 120 percent surge in diagnoses between 2002 and 2012.**[2]

Keep in mind these numbers only account for children who have been *identified* after being tested and then receiving a formal diagnosis. So the real number of kids with autism is likely somewhat higher. With each new promotion year, **the growing number of children with autism are becoming teens with autism**. That means they're entering your church youth ministry.

As with any special needs diagnosis, autism spectrum disorder is complex and requires a largely individualized approach. A broad range of learning styles, behaviors, disabilities, and abilities (that are sometimes unusual) fall under the ASD umbrella. And the degree of impairment varies widely. One individual with autism may require assistance with basic life skills while another needs little, if any, support. As a result, many high-functioning students with autism have more in common with their typically developing peers than with other kids sharing the same diagnosis. For this reason there is no one-size-fits-all solution for including students with ASD. Autism doesn't always show up in the form of a physical or intellectual disability. In fact, almost half (46%) of individuals identified with ASD have average or above average intelligence level.[3]

Oftentimes, autism presents itself in the form of awkward social interactions and unexpected behaviors. These attributes can present unique challenges for a youth ministry environment, where nearly every aspect of programming revolves around personal connection and relationship. But there is hope for kids like John who have autism, and for their student ministry leaders.

Is Inclusion Even Possible?

While "John" isn't his real name, John is a real student at a real church in suburban Atlanta, Georgia. When John transitioned out of children's ministry and into youth group, the student ministry team worried about including him.

But that was four years ago. John has since become an integral part of the same circle of boys, now sophomores in high school. One of John's small group leaders, Ben Nunes, reflects on the early days: "Before we figured out a few key strategies, there were weeks we spent more time managing John than doing anything else." But Nunes quickly points out, "John needed time to acclimate to us. And we needed time to figure out what makes him comfortable a well as how to avoid or overcome what makes him nervous."

Nunes acknowledges, "Interruptions and awkward moments still occur." But he quickly asserts that he would no longer call them interruptions or awkward moments, "It's just what happens with John." Everyone in the group has grown past the discomfort. The unexpected is now expected and rarely do John's "quirks" get noticed anymore. Nunes insists that the quality of the group's interactions have not been compromised. Instead, he contends that the guys have bonded partially due to the shared experiences that John has serendipitously created.

John's integration into the student ministry hasn't been without hiccups. Small group outings and youth group events nearly always pose a challenge. And the solution is different every time. Sometimes John participates after his parents have coached leaders through anticipated obstacles and prepared him for the new experience. Other times John will skip the event because his parents and leaders have determined he is not yet ready socially or developmentally. John is more likely to attend short, structured group events and forego the more fluid or open-ended get-togethers. And when John does come to extra activities, his father often comes along as an additional adult support.

John's small group leaders hope he can join the rest of the group on next year's overnight youth retreat. But the ministry team also appreciates that his parents have taken a thoughtful approach in years past, electing not to send John because he wasn't ready for sleepless nights and cafeteria-style serving lines. The small group leaders respect that John's parents have a good handle on their child's growth pace. And by sometimes taking the hard decisions off the shoulders of the student ministry team, John's parents consistently set everyone up for success.

Best Practices for Inclusion

For the past several years it's been my mission to help churches successfully include children with special needs. I've conducted dozens, if not hundreds, of interviews with ministry leaders and credentialed professionals working with individuals with disability. And I've hopped on planes to visit churches across the US, going into Sunday settings to see firsthand what's working when it comes to including kids with neurological differences. A number of best practices continually resurface in my research. And below are a few favorite ideas worth sharing. Please remember that every student with special needs is unique. **These strategies that work for one individual may not work for another who has an identical diagnosis.** And an approach that fails the first time can yield success after repetition. It's all about getting to know the student and trial and error. While these following ideas are shared with autism in mind, they are transferrable to a wide range of disabilities and unique needs.

1. Develop a good relationship with parents. When church leaders demonstrate a genuine desire to include a student with special needs, they increase the odds of having a healthy and trusting relationship with the parents. An honest line of open communication between the church and the family can be critical for success. Many problems can be solved (often before they happen) when a parent does not fear being turned away and shares more openly about their child's obstacles.

2. Prepare the student ahead of time. We all know that it's difficult to enjoy what's going on around us when we are preoccupied with worry. This is an ongoing problem for many students with autism because anxiety and autism often go hand-in-hand.[4] In fact, anxiety can be the root cause of undesirable behaviors sometimes associated with autism. If a student tends to run away, hide, or show visible signs of agitation around the time of a change, odds are high that the student is anxious about a current or upcoming activity. **With careful observation, leaders can usually identify the cause of the undesirable behavior and then prevent or resolve the trigger.** However, it is always smart to remove any element of surprise for the nervous student. Advance preparation eases worry and reduces the likelihood of negative behaviors whenever unfamiliar faces, different rooms, or new activities are going to be introduced.

The following tools and strategies may help some students:

- Offer an advance tour of ministry space and other relevant church environments.

- Send pictures and names of key faces the student can expect to see.

- Provide a map of the church campus, labeling rooms and highlighting travel routes.

- Create a visual schedule with activity times, locations, and brief descriptions.

- Use a stopwatch or visual timer as a countdown for current and upcoming activities.

3. Provide printed guidelines for each ministry setting. Every board game comes with a set of printed instructions. The instruction sheet establishes the purpose of the game and the rules for play. Ambiguity is removed and all players start with an equal understanding of what they can and cannot do during their turn. Some kids with neurodevelopmental disorders need the same type of instructions for "how to play" in the church youth group. **Concrete guidelines can help the student who does not catch on to the unwritten rules of play that are typically communicated through social cues.**

Because kids with ADHD, autism, anxiety, depression, OCD, and many other disabilities are simultaneously dealing with internal tension (e.g., overstimulation, hyperfocus, nervousness, impulsivity, physical pain, hyperactive "running motor"), they easily miss what's going on around them. A list of clearly stated "Do's and Don'ts" along with a simple objective statement for each ministry setting may seem insulting but is actually helpful for some students. Keep in mind that the rules should not be used as a way to shame or embarrass an individual who needs things spelled out literally or who requires regular reminders. In some cases it is best to provide the guidelines discreetly through email or private conversation.

4. Facilitate interaction for the student who struggles to communicate. While ministry leaders can't remove every obstacle, they can prompt and model interactions between the student with special needs and their peers. This often requires a leader to learn more about the communication abilities of a particular student and to create some out-of-the-box solutions. For example, a leader may learn that a student who rarely speaks during small group is actually an extrovert on social media. Odds are high that this silent kid in the corner will interact more with the small group via text or group chat. So in addition to asking discussion questions when the group is gathered, the leader also challenges group members to respond to posted discussion questions via text or group chat. So in addition to asking discussion questions when the group is gathered, the leader also challenges the group members to respond to posted discussion questions via text or a shared (and parent approved) chat app. This type of interaction is helpful for a student who:

- Processes auditory information at a slower pace (i.e., doesn't think fast on her feet)

- Struggles to articulate thoughts

- Speaks with inaudible, mumbled, or labored speech

- Experiences distraction or overstimulation in the live group setting

- Fails to interpret subtle, nonverbal, face-to-face communication

5. Remember that inclusion is more about a mind-set than a perfect set of strategies. Like John, not every student with special needs can successfully participate in *every* ministry activity. And that's okay. What the student with disability really needs from a youth group is a sense of belonging. Inclusion happens when an individual feels known and accepted for whom God created them to be.

> **What the student with disability really needs from a youth group is a sense of belonging.**

Discussion and Action Points

As you read this article, did a student's face come to mind? While reflecting on their unique traits or needs, create one action step to follow up based on these ideas.

Do you have a student with challenging behaviors possibly attributable to a disability? Many behavior dilemmas can be prevented or eliminated once you identify the "trigger." Take a sheet of paper and create three columns. In the middle column note the undesirable behavior. To the left, describe events preceding the incident, and to the right note what happened after or in response. Keep an ongoing log for recurring behaviors. Journaling the behaviors and surrounding facts will either help to identify the cause or serve as the starting point for solution-oriented conversations with parents.

Identify a student unable to do all the same activities as their peers. Write down two possible action steps to help them experience a sense of belonging inside the ministry.

Identify a knowledgeable person in your community whom you can approach for guidance. Good sources related to special needs inclusion are often:

> Speech language pathologists
>
> Occupational therapists
>
> Pediatric physical therapists
>
> Special education teachers
>
> Social workers[5]

―――

Part Two: Excerpts from Interviews with Katie Garvert Featured In "Including Teens with Special Needs" on theinclusivechurch.com

Question: Why is teen inclusion difficult?

Katie's Answer: First, the very nature of student ministry is social and relationship-driven. The typical student is really into their friends. The tool for life-change is shared experiences and conversation with other students. So, a good youth pastor is constantly thinking about how they can create an environment that invites interaction.

But for the student who has poor social skills or who struggles to communicate, the idea of conversation and interaction with others is not appealing. For some students with special needs, they can't think of anything they'd enjoy less than having to be social. And who blames them? No one enjoys doing things they aren't naturally good at.

Students with special needs can be easily misunderstood. One individual might be unfiltered, blurting out the first thought that pops into their head. Another student with disability struggles to form and express complete sentences. Both scenarios create tension for the student with special needs as well as their peers, who may be attempting to interact. Typically developing students sometimes react harshly in these awkward moments.

In general, teens don't exactly have the market cornered on emotional maturity. They're still developing. So, odds are high that a student with severe ADHD or high functioning autism has already had a number of uncomfortable peer encounters by the time they reach your youth ministry. Perhaps this student was even bullied by some of the others that show up at youth group. You can see why the very tool (social interaction) that a student ministry team uses may be the one thing that a student with special needs associates with failure.

Another reason teen inclusion can be a challenge is because parents and students with special needs often disagree on their goals for church participation. Let me illustrate this challenge: Just before anyone who has come through our special needs ministry promotes from children's ministry to student ministry, our leadership meets with each family. We bring the parents and student together along with someone from our ministry team. First, we ask parents to share their goals for their daughter or son's participation in the church youth group. Nearly always, we hear things like "be active in a small group;" "make quality friends;" and "participate in a student ministry mission trip." After parents have shared their desires, we then ask the student to talk about the student ministry experience they envision for themselves. And it is not uncommon for us to hear this response:

"Nothing. I don't want to be at church at all."

We dive a little deeper with the promoting student and the story that emerges is fairly predictable. For this student, moving up to the youth groups feels like a setup for failure. His or her memory bank isn't full of successful interactions in social situations. Most likely . . .

She isn't good at small talk.

He has difficulty talking about the interests of others.

She's already felt rejection from some of the same girls at school.

He thinks the youth group games are silly.

And to add to this list, nothing sounds worse than traveling on a mission trip, an experience full of unfamiliar environments and changes to their routine.

Mom and dad have their own goals for their son or daughter. And either consciously or subconsciously, the parents are pushing against the grain with their child. This push is causing even more resistance from the student. And as a ministry team, we feel it. (To the student's credit, they are probably more in tune with their differences and the realities that accompany them.) In situations like this, a church can easily feel like they are in a no-win situation. But it doesn't have to be that way.

Question: How does your church partner with parents?

Katie's Answer: We start by setting up a meeting where the parents, the promoting student, and someone from our ministry all come together to begin mapping out a plan for the teen. Parents share their goals and then the student tells us what they want (or don't want) out of the youth ministry experience.

It is during this meeting that a difference in goals may surface between the parents and the student. Our ministry leaders are prepared for this and if that tension is present, we want it to come out in this meeting. It's important for parents to see that their vision doesn't match what their student wants for themselves. This often creates an awkward moment, but we recognize it may be a pivotal moment for many reasons. We don't work to bridge the gap in goals and understanding in this same meeting but we do calmly share that this isn't the first time our church has worked through a similar challenge. Our ministry leader may convey that we aren't worried and ask the family to trust us to work toward a solution. It's really important to avoid the temptation to solve the problem in this same meeting because parents may need time to process the significance of the tension that emerged. We adjourn and schedule a follow-up time to talk with the parents alone, without the student.

In our second meeting, when only the parents are present, we address the apprehensions that surfaced in our previous time together and when the student was present. We explain that the student's spiritual growth is our church's priority, and this may be something new for the parents to consider. With discernment, our ministry team may address the fact that a desire for social growth is secondary. And in order for us (the church) to have influence with their son or daughter, we've got to create an accepting place for them. We're not going to put a child in a group or setting where they don't feel they can succeed. So, we may remove the idea of small group participation if the student can't get excited about it. We may also ask parents to table their goals for a mission trip for the time being. We want to get their son or daughter comfortable with spending two hours at church before we start talking about overnight trips. We often tell families to view our church's response as a "not now" rather than a "forever no".

> **We often tell families to view our church's response as a "not now" rather than a "forever no".**

Parents are usually supportive when they recognize our desire to provide a positive church experience for their child, just like we want for typically developing students. We help mom and dad understand that you can't connect with someone spiritually if they don't feel comfortable or don't feel like they're succeeding.

Before we leave this meeting, we ask parents for the following three commitments:

1. Require their student to attend our student ministry environment weekly. If participation is optional, our best efforts are likely to fail. Due to understandable anxiety, the student may prefer to stay home. Without making church attendance mandatory, we'll never get the chance for trial and error. The church can't force the student to come. But the parents can require the physical cooperation of their son or daughter.

2. Support our ministry team. We are going to try some new things with their student. We need the freedom to have some misses before we get it right. We are up front in explaining to the family that it might not be perfect in the beginning but our church leaders need their patience. We ask them not to get mad or give up until we've exhausted all of our ideas.

3. Commit to providing timely transportation for their student. Arriving late may mean their students misses the one thing we had planned to be their "success." And leaving early could cause the student to miss a key spiritual growth opportunity.

Question: What are some best practices your church has adopted related to including teens with special needs?

Katie's Answer: Most important, we recognize that God created our students with special needs as distinct individuals. We see our approach as allowing God to pursue each of them through the abilities and passions He gave them. We try to incorporate the following ideas or strategies into our approach with each student:

1. We help the student feel in control. Assuming parents have agreed to the requests I outlined previously, we invite the promoting student to a follow-up meeting with our ministry team. The student will come on his or her own and without the parents. This meeting gives our church the opportunity to show the student that we respect them as an individual. We start by acknowledging that our ministry team has already met with their parents and that the student's church participation is not optional. But just because church is mandatory for the student doesn't mean it has to be miserable. Right off the bat, our ministry team talks about the fact we are willing to make adjustments to their student ministry experience. We give the teen or pre-teen a say and if they are averse to being placed in a small group or particular ministry environment, we don't argue. We then go through a series of questions to figure out what the student is good at and what they enjoy.

2. We create jobs inside the student ministry. We look for ways the student can do what they love or can feel like they are making a contribution. For example, if we discover a student likes to create PowerPoint or Keynote presentations, we're going to ask him to build a visual presentation for our student pastor. We'll outline our needs and expectations and give this student a concrete deadline. If our student follows through, he may be asked to produce a visual presentation once a month, then twice a month and so on. This student is receiving a "reward" by seeing their work utilized at the weekly student ministry event. A routine is emerging (so important!) all while this student has a growing sense of worth and success.

When we create tasks or jobs for our students we are strategically creating opportunities for their spiritual growth. We have a number of students with special needs running lights and sound or performing some sort of task on the production team. These students are sitting inside the tech booth for the duration of the student ministry experience, hearing the Bible-rich content we want them to hear. And they are having a shared experience, in a corporate sense, with the rest of the youth group. But it doesn't end there. Just after the large group experience concludes and as other students are going to their respective small groups, the production team has a debrief meeting. The adult volunteer running the tech booth (brilliantly) invites group discussion on what went right or what needs to improve for next week's production. The students helping in the booth are often eager to weigh in on technical topics, meanwhile growing comfortable interacting with each other. The production team then closes out their meeting with a Bible-devotion, as would be the case for any ministry meeting at the church. It just so happens that the tech team's devotion will always piggyback off the topic covered during large group. And the brief group questions may be from the small group geaders' discussion materials.

Do you catch what's happening here? There's a small group that doesn't know it's a small group happening inside our tech booth. Kids who didn't want to participate in a small group are happily taking part of the learning and dialogue happening inside the tech booth. While it may be untraditional, we see our student ministry production team as a small group.

3. We try to solve problems before they become problems. Some students can and want to be part of a more traditional small group. It's our ministry's job to navigate their placement. Obviously the "job" approach or tech team assignment doesn't work for every student with special needs. This is especially true for girls. Oftentimes in our early conversation with a female student, we'll learn that she is uncomfortable around the "social girls" whom she perceives to be boy crazy or shallow.

We've found success by pairing this type of student with an adult small group leader who likes to explore topics outside of pop stars and trendy fashion. This leader might be someone who throws out big ideas related to social justice or theology. While the student with learning differences may not always track with the group discussion, she isn't going to be boiling in anger listening to the latest teen-scene gossip. In addition, we've placed the student with a leader who is more naturally sensitive to this student's unique life experiences. And we're going to work with that leader, providing any coaching that might be needed in order to provide an accepting, safe group dynamic that invites this student's participation. Our hope is that by taking an intentional and proactive approach, we've prevented some problematic group dynamics that sometimes occur around kids with special needs.

4. We look for opportunities to multiply our own success. So, now we've got students inside the tech booth that are mentoring the newbies on sound, lights, etc. Some of these mentors are the same students who would have rather severed an arm than get involved in our church's student ministry. And now these teens, many with special needs, are in their element, coming to church on their own accord, and investing in peers who are serving alongside them. It's really moving when you look out each week during the various youth events and see some students in the oddest places . . . and then you realize that the odd task you noticed some student doing is really the vehicle for his or her spiritual growth.

How the church defines inclusion for each student with a disability is going to vary. And as a child ages through adolescence, it may require more ingenuity and creativity to facilitate their meaningful participation in the church. But this differentiation shouldn't surprise us because the church experience for typical adults is largely differentiated by ability, interest, and unique needs. Not every adult sings in the choir, serves on the benevolence committee or attends the midweek Bible study on marriage. Different people do different things. And no one-way of plugging in or serving in the church is more beneficial or valuable than the other. The same thing is true for our students with special needs. And it's our church's responsibility, in partnership with parents, to clear the path so that God can pursue our teens through the abilities and passions he's already given them.

The big-picture goal of a church's special needs ministry is to facilitate a sense of belonging inside the bigger body of Christ. Our best indicator of success is when we see a student with special needs feeling accepted, comfortable and open to the church's influence in their life.

Appendix 1.1
Tips for Loving the Family Through the Diagnosis

Avoid common and well-meaning sentiments that may come across as dismissive. Families share that the following phrases often do *not* provide comfort:

> *"God doesn't give us more than we can handle."*
>
> *"Special needs children are a blessing."*
>
> *"God chose your family for this child."*
>
> *"Everything happens for a reason."*
>
> *Any statement that begins with "At least . . ."*

Quote Bible verses sparingly. Hearing a Bible verse such as Romans 8:28 can feel like a trite attempt to put a bandage over the pain.

Refrain from offering unknown assurances unless you have experienced something similar.

Request permission from the family before you reveal the diagnosis to others.

Do not suggest that either parent join a support group until they have expressed an interest.

Give Disability Visibility

Wear official autism awareness jewelry, lapel pins, and lanyard ribbons. Order these and other visible signs of support through www.SupportStore. com or www.AutismLink.com.

Celebrate Autism Awareness Month. Post facts or related tips on the church website or in a prominent area of the church. With permission, feature the story of a child with autism.

Plug in children with disability into visible places in the children's ministry. Assign a child with special needs a memorized line in a skit or the job of carrying the flag during VBS assembly.

Invite parents of children with disabilities to be a part of the children's ministry advisory team.

Arrange for a pediatric therapist or special needs professional to speak to a Moms-n-More church group. Ask the speaker to address developmental milestones while providing autism education.

Invite parents of children with a disability to share their family's story in various congregational settings.

Encourage ministry groups within the church to adopt service projects supporting the special needs ministry. Arrange for an adult fellowship group to host an Easter egg hunt, Christmas party, or respite event for children with special needs.

Adopt a one-time service project with a tie to disability. Contact local support organizations for ideas. Designate the project as a family ministry or outreach event.

Sponsor a local special needs "family fun" day along with other area churches.

Arrange for and publicize group outings to special needs friendly community events. Find sensory-friendly film days at a local theater or disability designated events offered by museums, zoos, and sports teams.

Appendix 7.1
Policies and Volunteer
Training Topics

Because every church will vary in their church mission, available resources, service and programming schedule, space, and local public school guidelines, no one set of policies will apply to any two special needs ministries. What follows is a list of common issues that are best addressed in a ministry handbook or as part of a volunteer training event.

Virtually every issue covered in a preschool or children's ministry handbook should be covered in a volunteer handbook and training event. We do not repeat many of those important topics here. What follows are examples of wording and ideas for how a church might address issues unique to special needs ministry.

Guiding Statements Example

Part of the purpose of having ministry policies is to provide staff, lay leaders, and volunteers a road map for solving anticipated challenges. By its nature, accommodation is more individual-specific for participants with special needs than for typically developing children and students. Because we can't predict every possible need or issue that might arise, we stress here the importance of conversations when addressing problems and developing solutions. Often, the ministry's leadership is required to exercise careful discernment and judgment when determining how to apply the guidelines of the ministry.

We believe in God's value for every human life. And we believe that Jesus desires a personal relationship with every person, regardless of their abilities or disabilities. Out of these beliefs, the special needs ministry was created to facilitate an appropriate accommodation plan for the individual with additional needs while working within the policies and resources of the church. The desire of our church's special needs ministry is to partner with parents in developing plans to appropriately accommodate each participant in the church setting. Ensuring the safety of any child (with or without special needs) and of those around them is the top priority of our church.

Screening Requirements

The same screening policies for a church's preschool, children's, and student ministries should be applied inside the special needs ministry. All volunteers and ministry leaders should be required to undergo an appropriate background check, ensuring all prospective caregivers have no prior record that would compromise their ability to serve reliably and effectively in a ministry environment. Any convictions related to sexual abuse would automatically disqualify a person from service. Persons with any history of sexual misconduct may use their gifts in other areas of the church, outside of working with children and individuals with special needs.

The church also may require prospective volunteers to complete a brief application, perhaps offering reasons they want to serve in the ministry and providing references. Calling references can be a wise and effective way to learn about a person's personal and professional history. Such conversations may reveal information that does not show up in a standard background check. I highly recommend taking this extra step to discern who will serve participants with special needs. Statistically speaking, individuals with special needs are more susceptible to abuse.[1] Any time an individual with special needs shows signs of abuse, everyone in their circle is under a cloud of suspicion. Reference checks protect participants and protect the church from utilizing the services of individuals who have, in the past, demonstrated themselves to be unsafe around children.

Two-Person Rule for Caregivers

This policy is common inside most church preschool and children's ministry settings. The policy requires that two unmarried, screened, and approved adults always be present during church-provided childcare. At no time would any child or any number of children be left alone without any caregiver or with only a single adult caregiver. Married adults may serve together but for the purpose of this rule, they do not count as two separate adults. As with many other policies, this rule prevents the probability and perception of abuse.

Many churches will not permit parents to leave their child inside a ministry setting until two unmarried adults have arrived and are prepared to supervise. This policy is very important to enforce in cases where a parent drops off their child early, leaving them unattended in any part of church, prior to the workers' arrival. If the individual is older, perhaps even an adult with an intellectual disability, it is still unwise and dangerous to permit the individual to remain in the ministry setting unsupervised. The two-person rule ensures adequate and safe supervision. In order to protect the safety of such an individual and for the purposes of establishing good risk management practices, the church may need to inform and remind parents of the policy as well as restrict access to the ministry environment until caregivers are present and prepared to supervise.

Training Requirements

Some ministries require that no one can serve as a one-on-one aide or inside a special needs ministry environment until they have completed the necessary training. The training may be special needs specific or it can be whatever training is offered to the preschool ministry and children's ministry volunteers (many of the topics covered in this section are or should be covered in typical ministry handbooks and training sessions.) In addition, some ministries may require that inside every ministry environment there is at least one person with six months or more of leadership service. In other words, you wouldn't have a class where there are two "newbie" volunteers.

Intake Process and First-Time Participants and Guests

Each church should decide how they will gather information for each participant with special needs. I strongly recommend *requiring* the completion of an intake interview and form for every individual who utilizes the services of the special needs ministry. However, I can understand where some churches would opt to accept and place participants who perhaps show up unannounced and without the full completion of the intake process and paperwork.

Some churches require that each child's intake documents be updated annually and further state that failure of parents to do so by a certain date may prevent the child's participation in the church environment. While this may seem harsh, it can be a great policy for protecting the child and everyone involved in their accommodation plan. For example, knowing the signs of an impending seizure for a particular child or learning about new calming strategies that are helpful as a student goes through hormone changes can be key information for ensuring the continued success of the student.

Sensitive Parent Conversations

Personally, I believe volunteers are generally not the best choice for addressing sensitive topics with parents. Leadership staff needs to determine and communicate who is responsible for informing parents when any new or additional requirements are not met. A ministry manual or volunteer training event should spell out instructions for pulling in the designated leaders to initiate parent conversations when difficult situations arise. Having a parent show up and drop off a child when the intake process remains incomplete is an example of a scenario best suited for a leader-led (and not volunteer-led) conversation. Along the same lines, a ministry leader needs to be designated for making placement decisions for first-time guests and visitors. It is important that ministry volunteers understand these processes and know how to handle situations that are likely to arise.

Toileting and Diapering

It is extremely important for a church to determine its policy on toileting and diapering and to stick to it for the purpose of preventing both the perception and probability of abuse. I have become aware of situations where a church has been shielded from both merited and unmerited accusations because they had and followed preventative policies. Below are three toileting and diapering approaches I most often see churches adopt for the purpose of serving children with special needs:

1. Parents assume responsibility.

For children over a certain age (usually around age four or five), parents are required to handle all bathroom needs. Some churches provide a family restroom adjacent to or nearby the special needs ministry environments. One church even installed a large shower inside their nearby family restroom to help with any emergency clean-ups. Parents may be asked or reminded to toilet their child at drop-off. If a need were to arise for a diaper change or pit-stop during programming, the parents would be notified via a text to their cell phone or by a pager to come tend to their child. This policy always receives blessings from insurance companies and is the most conservative approach for a church. A secondary benefit to this policy is that prospective volunteers are less reluctant to serve because these duties will never fall under their responsibility.

I am aware of several churches with comprehensive special needs inclusion programs that have adopted this policy. In every case, the policy was adopted only after extensive conversation with the church's insurance company and/or legal advisor.

2. Church hires a nurse through an outside agency.

For churches that can afford the added expense of hiring a nurse through a third-party agency, this is a wonderful option. This hired nurse can tend to toileting/diapering needs during church programming. And the nurse's employer (not the church, but the contracted agency) assumes the responsibility for screening, training, bonding, and insuring the medical professional.

3. A designated church employee assumes responsibility.

For this approach the special needs ministry coordinator or other approved and designated ministry leader (always a female) handles all toileting/diapering needs of the participants. A second female adult is required to be present during all diaper changes or bathroom visits. Parents and volunteers are notified of this policy. Parents may choose not to have the designated church employee tend to their child's bathroom needs and instead handle those needs themselves. No volunteers are ever tasked with toileting/diapering requirements during regular church programming.

Snacks and Allergies; Use of EpiPens

Restricted diets and food sensitivities seem to be more common among children with special needs. Churches tend to handle this issue differently. Some churches offer a different snack inside the special needs ministry environments (perhaps they offer gluten-free pretzels or dried cereals, whereas the typical children's ministry settings offer a popular, less expensive cracker containing gluten). Other special needs ministries offer no snacks, fearing cross contamination and the increased difficulty for volunteers to remember which child gets which snack. Some ministries require that the child bring a carefully labeled snack from home.

How a church communicates a child's allergies and dietary restrictions is important. It's also important to make a distinction between whether a child has a food sensitivity or a true allergy that could result in an anaphylaxis reaction. Will the child's allergies be noted on their nametag? On a list posted in the room? The church may also need to determine if and how it will handle the use of epinephrine autoinjectors (a common trade name for this device is EpiPen).

On a related note, crafts may need to be planned around food sensitivities because touching products containing certain allergens or gluten may also be harmful. While thinking about the children in your care, be sure to review the ingredients of each brand of modeling clay or putty, glue, inkpads, and paints.

For the purposes of understanding common food intolerances, I've included the following set of definitions, which may be helpful to include inside a special needs ministry manual.

GFCF (Gluten-Free, Casein-Free)—This diet may be part of a child's treatment plan for any number of diagnoses, or vital to their physical well-being.

GF (Gluten-Free)—This diet is often associated with medical and health requirement for individuals diagnosed with Celiac Disease. Many people without Celiac Disease opt to adopt a gluten-free diet for other notable health benefits.

Celiac Disease—Refers to a genetic and autoimmune disease where the body attacks itself when exposed to gluten, which is found in wheat, barley, rye, and many brands of oats.

Casein-Free—Refers to a diet eliminating a naturally occurring protein commonly found in dairy products, like milk, cheese, and yogurt.

Food Allergies—A hypersensitivity to a dietary substance (e.g., nuts) causing an overreaction of the immune system, which may lead to severe physical symptoms.

Anaphylaxis—A serious allergic reaction that is rapid in onset and may cause death. Symptoms and signs of an allergic reaction include hives, redness of the skin, tightness of the throat, breathing problems, and/or decrease in blood pressure. Common causes of anaphylaxis include food, medication, insect stings, latex, and occasionally but rarely, exercise. Anaphylactic reactions are generally considered a medical emergency.

EpiPen®—A trade name for one type of epinephrine autoinjector. Epinephrine shots deliver a measured dose of medication to treat acute allergic reactions and the onset of anaphylactic shock. Auvi-Q® is another name for this type of medical device. Individuals at heightened risk for anaphylaxis reactions should carry these types of devices with them at all times. Caregivers may need training to understand how and when to administer an injection.

Behavior Management

It is often helpful for a church to bring in someone with experience in special education or behavioral therapy to provide tips for effective behavior management. It is extremely important that volunteers are coached to avoid handling a child physically as much as humanly possible. Physical restraint is very controversial and in some areas illegal. If volunteers see signs that a child's behavior is headed in an undesirable direction, every effort should be made to contain the situation before physical force is required. Parents may need to be paged for their immediate attention and help so the need for physical restraint by volunteers or staff can be avoided. Physical force would be an absolute last resort and used only to prevent or minimize imminent physical harm. We talk about managing undesirable behavior in greater detail in chapter 8.

Some children do benefit from deep pressure and hugs to meet their unique sensory needs. This is something that the volunteers need to understand for each child and receive parent approval before applying or trying themselves. As a general rule, physical touch should not be applied in any way beyond what is appropriate for a typically developing child.

It may be helpful to provide the following guidelines of behavior management:

The Rs of Behavior Management

Request a child stop disruptive or harmful behavior.
Give children the freedom to fidget; pick battles.

Redirect misbehaving children. Ask the child a question on an unrelated subject to break the focus or the conflict. Provide the child an alternative such as a toy, and ask the child to help with a task in another part of the room.

Remove obstacles. Recognize the underlying cause. If the child is tired, suggest a chill-out time on a beanbag. If the child is hungry, provide a small snack. If a certain toy is causing constant conflict, tell the toy "bye-bye" and put it out of eyesight for everyone.

Responsibility for instilling consequences or hard conversations should always be with adults and never with teen helpers. Oftentimes, a ministry team designates one or two specific adult leaders to handle behavior challenges that have escalated to the point of requiring consequences and/or parent involvement.

Parent Communication

Parents of children with special needs are accustomed to receiving negative reports on their child, especially as it pertains to behavior. An important reminder for special needs volunteers is the importance of being flexible and laid-back. There are so many factors driving a child's behavior which we discuss at length in chapter 8. Volunteer conversations with parents are best when not loaded with bad reports about a child's behavior. If a parent inquires about a child's behavior and demeanor during his or her church experience, there are times that candid feedback can be helpful. But, the ministry needs to have an established and positive relationship with the family so that when anything negative is shared, the parents know that their child isn't at risk of being "expelled" from the ministry. On the other hand, special needs ministry volunteers and leaders can never provide enough affirmation. As a result, negative feedback should be avoided to a large degree. And when it is necessary, a designated ministry leader should ideally be the one to convey that sensitive information.

Positive parent communication helps to strengthen, build, and protect the growing relationship between the volunteer and the parents of a participating child. Parents of children with special needs are like all parents—they love hearing how their child participated in class, something cute they said to a teacher, or how their child helped a neighbor during craft time.

And don't forget that anytime a child engages during the Bible lesson or shows evidence of spiritual growth, these moments should be communicated to and celebrated with the parents.

One ministry leader shared with me that some parents in her ministry didn't think their child was capable of growing spiritually before they came to church. These parents were just thankful for a place to provide babysitting while they attended their own small group and worship. But after they realized their child with significant cognitive delays was engaged and learning during the Bible story time in the church's special needs environment, the parents took a more active approach to Bible teaching inside the home.

Volunteers should never underestimate their power to encourage and even influence parents, especially during child checkout.

During their time together or other significant moments, the special needs ministry leaders may text a picture directly to the parents. (Be sure not to take pictures and send it to others without permission!) Few things bring as much joy to parents as seeing evidence of their child's positive experience inside the church.

> Volunteers should never underestimate their power to encourage and even influence parents, especially during child checkout.

Participant Privacy and Confidentiality

It's incredibly helpful when families reveal pertinent information about their child's unique needs and diagnosis. And the church owes it to these families to honor their decision to disclose relevant facts by protecting their privacy. The medical profession and education system mandate privacy. Special needs leaders, volunteers, and buddies should share participant information strictly on a "need to know" basis and only inside the confines of the special needs ministry. Failure to respect and guard a family's right to privacy may result in the immediate dismissal of a volunteer.

Some churches require volunteers to sign a covenant vowing not to reveal any information about a child's needs, behaviors, or family issues to anyone not working directly with the individual and especially outside the ministry. Failure to honor this policy will result in the immediate release of the volunteer's service to the special needs ministry.

Medical Treatment

Many churches outline in their ministry policies, handbooks, and volunteer job descriptions that volunteers are not permitted to dispense or apply medication. Along the same lines, many churches prohibit their volunteers and leaders from rendering medical treatment. If a participant requires ongoing medical assistance, it would be necessary for them to provide their own medical aide to accompany them while participating in church environments and events.

In emergency medical situations, the ministry documents may spell out that ministry leaders and caregivers may call 911.

Safety Emergencies and Medical Emergencies

The ministry leadership needs to determine the first steps of response and contacts for anticipated emergencies. Many emergencies can be prevented. And for the unavoidable emergencies, following a response plan may contain or minimize any undesirable outcomes. Perhaps one of the most important reasons to hold a special needs ministry training event is for the purpose of preparing volunteers to respond appropriately in emergency situations. Each church's response plan will be unique, factoring in considerations including local laws, the advice of area law enforcement, the capabilities of the church's security team, and the counsel of the church's insurance provider.

For information on seizures, recognizing warning signs, and preparing for an appropriate response, the Daniel Jordan Fiddle Foundation and www.djfiddlefoundation.com has produced an excellent education piece. See the following web address to access a helpful brochure for volunteers: djfiddle-foundation.org/news/attach/DJF-EpilepsyBrochure.pdf.

Teen Servant Responsibilities and Limitations

Churches that have the most successful partnerships with teens provide concrete guidelines for their student helpers, removing ambiguity and clarifying their responsibilities. Teen helpers are subject to the leadership of every adult working inside any ministry environment. Teens are assistants and have little or no authority for making decisions or changes to a participant's accommodation plan. Teens should never instill any type of punishment or consequences for behavior problems. Teens can and should work through the first three "Rs" of behavior management (request, redirect, and remove, explained earlier in this appendix piece). However, teens should refer problems to designated adults when the need for further action arises. Teens should also refrain from offering any negative feedback on a student to their parents. All sensitive conversations should be handled by adult ministry leaders and never teen helpers. Teens should also guard the privacy of the participants they serve and never reveal the diagnoses or other issues to people without the need to know or outside the ministry. Teen class helpers and teen buddies should also refer significant conflicts among each other to adult ministry leaders.

Special Needs/Disability Etiquete

Consider covering basic pointers of disability etiquette.

Disability Etiquette Pointers

Don't Say: Special needs child
Do Say: Child with special needs

Don't Say: Autistic child
Do Say: Child with autism

Don't Say: Downs kid, Down syndrome child
Do Say: Child with Down syndrome

Don't Say: Disabled person
Do Say: Person with a disability, or differently abled

Don't Say: Mental retardation, or mentally retarded
Do Say: Person with intellectual disability

Speak directly to the person with the disability. Even if the person has limited communication skills and utilizes an interpreter, look at and speak to the person with the disability.

Do not force an individual to look you in the eye. Recognize that neurological disorders may make an individual uncomfortable with eye contact.

Take the parents' lead. Use their same terminology when introducing the child and family to others.

For more guidance, see the online article: "On Greeting Persons with Disabilities: A Suggestion Manual for Ushers and Greeters" from Discipleship Ministries of the United Methodist Church.

Parent Presence on Campus

Some churches require that parents remain on the church campus at all times while the church cares for the child. By having close access to a child's parent or guardian (in terms of physical distance), parents are able to respond in a timely fashion as specific needs may arise. This is especially helpful in cases where the church neither tends to the bathroom needs nor offers medical treatment to the individual with special needs.

For events such as respite and Vacation Bible School, the policy requiring parents to remain on campus may be altered. However, it is for those reasons that the care offered during those settings (respite, VBS, retreats) often requires the presence professionally trained service providers (e.g., registered nurse) as well as a greater level of training for all caregivers. A church should work closely with their insurance provider when developing the policies and practices for hosting respite events.

Parent Help in the Ministry

While one of the central objectives of the special needs ministry is to enable parents to attend church and receive their own spiritual nourishment, some churches have found it useful to require periodic parent service. This is a church-specific determination and depends completely on the needs and culture of each particular ministry. Churches that require ministry service of parents of typically developing children may also want to require the same of parents of children with special needs.

One special needs ministry leader shared that the parent support of her church's ministry shifted significantly after parents were required to offer occasional service themselves. Instead of feeling disappointment for what the special needs ministry was or wasn't doing for their child, families were able to see the great lengths to which the volunteers were going to facilitate each child's success. Parents began feeling and expressing heartfelt appreciation to the volunteers and the dissention that had begun to emerge quickly dissipated.

Advance Notice and Accommodation Limitations

Some churches require advance notice when a family plans to attend or not attend church. It can help tremendously with staffing and space issues when parents call ahead and as their plans change. It is also acceptable for a church to require advance notice before ensuring accommodation, especially as it relates to one-time events (not regularly recurring weekend or Sunday-morning programming). Churches may also limit certain types of accommodation to predetermined times. For example, for space or staffing purposes, a church might offer the special needs environment only during one worship service. It is in everyone's best interest for the church to be adequately prepared for students who require the assistance of trained staff and/or a space with enhanced security features. Those resources may have limited availability and for that reason, requiring advance arrangements or limiting the church's accommodation options may be necessary.

If a church requires advance notice for accommodation or limits the hours of accommodation, this information must be posted publicly and communicated regularly. It is important that parents aren't caught off guard and that the process is easy for them to secure accommodation arrangements.

Mandatory Reporting

Each state has laws requiring certain people to report concerns of child abuse and neglect. While some states require all people to report their concerns, many states identify specific professionals as mandated reporters; these often include social workers, medical and mental health professionals, teachers, and childcare providers. In some cases, the laws apply to those providing care in a church setting. Specific procedures are usually established for mandated reporters to make referrals to child protective services. For better or for worse, most churches will at some point or another have a situation that requires investigation related to mandatory reporting requirements.[2] Make sure you know the federal and state laws that apply to your church.

Adapting Teaching for Special Needs

It's great if someone with experience modifying curriculum in the school system can offer a few quick tips.

Appendix 7.2
Teen Volunteer Training Event

Teen volunteers can be one of your ministry's most prized assets if they are trained and set up appropriately. Below is an idea outline for topics to cover in a teen training event. You will want to tweak the rules and stories to fit the culture and approved policies of your church. For a shorter training session, provide some of the below pointers in writing and require prospective volunteers to sign a document acknowledging they agree to the following guidelines.

Be sure to interject humorous side notes and funny role-playing into a teen training event. Teens love variety and attention! Recruit a couple of outgoing students to role-play suggested scenarios. While the content is serious, you can lead a training event with a light-hearted and fun approach. You'll know you are succeeding when you generate a few laughs among the students while fueling their excitement about becoming part of a meaningful ministry.

Special Needs Ministry Service Is a Calling

Share relevant example stories; Pose questions and invite dialogue from trainees.

Who is impacted by a church's children's ministry?

Why is this environment important to help people experience Christ? (Kids, parents, volunteers)

We can be a positive or negative influence on every person we come in contact with in the ministry.

Serving as a volunteer in a special needs environment isn't for everyone (Romans 12:4–8).

It's okay to decide that serving in this ministry doesn't match your gifts.

Role-play scenarios with outgoing students.

Invite training participants to guess which scenario is a good/bad reason to serve:

> Example #1: Place to hang out with boyfriend or gossip with best friend
>
> Example #2: Passionate about helping children experience Jesus' love

Special Needs Service Is a Job

The teachers you work with may give references on you in college and job applications.

You will have a "boss"—your manager is your classroom lead teacher.

Role-play reassignment or as Donald Trump says, "You're fired." (Have fun with this!)

> Example #1: Lead teacher makes a request of a teen. Teen demonstrates respect versus disrespect.
>
> Example #2: Not paying attention to children.

Job Description: Tasks teens are expected to help with:

- Providing individual help during crafts and other activities
- Keeping track of participants through transitions and in different settings
- Setting up for the next activity
- Keeping the room clean
- Preparing participant's take-home materials (e.g., VBS)

Alert your class teacher to your scheduling conflicts (arriving late, leaving early, etc.).

Why teen service is unique and especially helpful:

- Kids look up to teens, view them as "cool."
- Teens can often relate to and engage kids better than adults.
- Teen helpers can make learning more fun.

Safety

Perception is reality. We do things to be safe and to appear safe.

Physical handling of children can be good and bad.

No grabbing or jerking a child who is misbehaving.

No horseplay or piggyback rides.

Only teens over the age of fifteen can pick up children ages three and under.

Teens should never be alone with a child except when transitioning in public areas, in plain view.

Don't encourage children to sit in your lap—especially male helpers!

Toileting and Diapering

No toileting/diapering by any teens of any participants with special needs.

Handling Misbehaving Children

Role-play: Act out one or two common types of misbehavior and how the teen helpers should handle it.

The Rs of Behavior Management

Request a child to stop disruptive or harmful behavior. Give children the freedom to fidget; pick battles.

Redirect misbehaving children. Ask the child a question on an unrelated subject to break the focus or the conflict. Provide the child an alternate toy. Ask the child to help with a task in another part of the room.

Remove obstacles. Recognize the underlying cause. If the child is tired, suggest a chill-out time on a beanbag. If the child is hungry, provide him a small snack. If a certain toy is causing constant conflict, tell the toy "bye-bye" and put it out of eyesight for everyone.

Responsibility for instilling consequences or hard conversations should always be with adults. Teens should not be the ones to create "time-outs" for the child. Teens are never to talk to parents about behavior challenges.

Conflict between Teens

Allow the class leader to address conflicts between teen helpers.

Do's and Don'ts

No cell phone use.

No pictures, no texting pictures of kids, no posting pictures to Facebook.

Explain privacy issues. (For more on this topic, see 7.1.)

No carrying children; no piggyback rides.

Don't switch your class assignment without clearing it with the ministry director.

Do wear a church-issued nametag so that teachers and parents know you are an approved worker.

Do protect the privacy of child and family.

Check-In

Don't let parents leave a child with you without going through proper check-in procedures.

Checkout

Only authorized adult teachers may release participants to parents.

Do not interfere with conversations between the adult teachers and parents picking up their children.

Don't solicit babysitting jobs at checkout.

Allergies and Medical Issues

Define Anaphylaxis and discuss importance of allergy notifications.

Briefly discuss recognizing and responding to a seizure.

Do not ever administer medications to a child.

Go over an emergency response procedure.

Transitions and Taking Children outside of Classrooms

Transitions need to be carefully orchestrated so that each child is visually followed between settings.

Make sure all children are identified with adhesive name tags in case they are lost during transition.

Classroom Visitors

Don't allow parent visitors or other visitors in the room without lead teacher's approval.

Don't invite your friends to visit your classroom.

Confidentiality

Only discuss the following with relevant ministry leaders and only on a "need to know" basis: behavior issues, medical issues or special needs diagnoses, and problems in a child's home.

Abuse Prevention and Reporting

A brief mention may be required as church settings can be considered a "mandatory reporting" entity. This is a good time to cover the signs of abuse, the legal requirements for what to do when those signs are recognized, and who to tell/not to tell.

Impact Story or Video

Be sure to end the training on a positive and inspiring note. Feature a teen volunteer's story talking about the benefits of their service. Or invite a parent to share how a teen serving inside the ministry built a meaningful relationship with and made a difference for their child with special needs. If this is a new area of ministry, build a vision. Through a story or a shared vision, answer the questions:

> Why is it worth it to serve?
>
> How did this experience shape my life?
>
> How can my contribution bring meaning in the lives of the individuals or families I'm serving?

Appendix 7.3
Church Greeter/Host
Training Event

The purpose of this type of training is to equip the first faces at the church's information desk, welcome center, and key entry points. People who serve as parking lot greeters are often included because they may be the first person a family encounters on a church campus. Keep in mind that a physical or intellectual disability often becomes a challenge the minute the family's car door opens in the church parking lot. When a physical disability is involved, the family will likely need assistance in figuring out how to get their child who can't walk at all or can't walk comfortably into the church building. When an intellectual disability is involved, the family may require help calming the child who has suddenly realized he or she is going to a new and unfamiliar place. It is not unusual in situations like this for the anxiety to surface in the form of an undesirable behavior. And how the guy directing traffic in your church parking lot, along with every other person in a host or greeter-type role, responds can be the difference in whether or not that family stays and learns about Jesus.

What follows are my notes from a training event for church greeters and children's ministry hosts at Grace Church in Greenville, South Carolina. The audience also included the front-line volunteers who welcome and place first-time visitors into Sunday-morning small groups as well as children's ministry coaches who frequently respond to unique needs during Sunday morning programming. The sixty-minute training was informative and well received by the listeners, many of whom had no prior knowledge of the church's special needs ministry. Feel free to customize this event to fit your church culture and needs.

Special Needs Ministry Overview

The church's hospitality coordinator started the event by introducing and interviewing the special needs ministry leaders. The hospitality team leader posed the following questions to the interviewed special needs team members. (I have provided their answers in cases where it may be helpful.)

Question: How did you get involved in the church's special needs ministry?

Question: How do you define special needs in terms of ministry and this church? **Answer:** Any need a family member may have that requires some forethought in order to ensure that the family's church experience is meaningful and safe. This can include severe allergies, medical issues, or cognitive differences.

Question: What happens when a first-time guest notifies us that their child has special needs? **Answer:** The family is introduced to the children's ministry host team, who asks the parents to complete a special needs intake form. After a quick assessment, the children's ministry host or special needs coach may assign the child to the best environment for that morning. Then later, the children's ministry and special needs team will follow up with the family and together develop a plan for long-term inclusion.

Question: What should a greeter do/say if they suspect a new guest has an undisclosed disability? **Answer:** The greeter should not press the issue of a disability with the family. The greeter may want to discreetly privately notify the children's ministry team of their observations, with the intent of facilitating a successful and safe church experience for the family.

Question: What options does our church provide for special needs inclusion? **Answer:** (The special needs ministry team shared about the church's options for a special needs buddy as well as a specially-designed special needs classroom. The difference between the two accommodation options was explained as well as the factors that helped to determine which option was best for a particular participant.)

Question: Could a greeter ask parents to recommend an age group in which they would like to see their child with special needs assigned? **Answer:** It is best for the hospitality and welcome team members to avoid asking questions or engaging in a conversation about the child's placement. The children's ministry leaders and special needs coaches often take a number of factors into account before assigning a child to a certain church environment. And those parent conversations can sometimes require delicate diplomacy!

Terminology and Tone

Phrasing and terminology related to special needs can be very sensitive. Grace Church's special needs ministry leader, Emily McGowan (a former special education teacher), offers some general pointers:

Take the parents' lead. Use the same terminology when talking with the family or introducing them to others. If they don't use the word "disability" or say "special needs," then we don't use those terms either.

Always use person-first language. For example, say "child with Down syndrome" or "child with autism." Do **not** say "Downs kid" or "autistic child."

Do not refer to the family as a "special needs family."

When paging other team members, do not say, "I have a special needs family here." Simply say, "I have a family I would like you to meet."

Do not place a visiting child in a special needs classroom. A special needs placement would only be assigned if parents have comfortably shared about child's disability or need for special accommodation.

Be mindful of tone of voice. A family affected by special needs will likely pick up on their host's stress or concerns.

It is important to convey that the church cares more about the child and the family than the disability.

Parent Experience

The hospitality coordinator for Grace Church provided the audience the opportunity to better understand families affected by special needs by interviewing two families of children with special needs. The training leader asked questions, which follow, guiding each set of parents through a short synopsis of their family's story. The five- to ten-minute dialogue was incredibly moving. The audience heard how each family's interactions inside the church and the special needs ministry had impacted the spiritual growth of their entire family. Conveying her gratitude for Grace Church, one mother shared of the meaningful interactions she and her husband experienced when they first started attending the church with their daughter, who has autism.

Interview Questions

- Tell us about your family?

- How is parenting a child with special needs different than parenting a typical child?

- If you were visiting a church for the first time and from the perspective of a parent of a child with special needs, what would you hope to see?

- How has the special needs ministry of our church impacted your family?

- How can we be a more welcoming church for families affected by special needs?

As each family wrapped up their interview, the host coordinator invited them to give examples of how an interaction with someone inside the church could be perceived as positive or negative. The audience learned that comments and questions that may seem inconsequential are often significant to a family affected by special needs.

The interviewed families shared that every touch point with volunteers, staff, and other church members offered affirmation and acceptance. Each of the interviewed parents also shared how they had become active volunteers themselves in other areas of ministry inside the church. The listening audience of hosts and greeters could now better understand the important role they play in creating similar experiences for new or families affected by special needs.

Appendix 7.4
Volunteer Opportunities
Other Than Childcare

Lead music in special needs ministry setting (guitar, expressive singer with CD player).

Prepare art for classroom crafts and activities.

Create sensory walls or tactile murals for special needs environments.

Coordinate master schedule of ministry volunteers.

Design and launch a special needs ministry website.

Produce graphic design for marketing pieces and website.

Photograph or video program events for church social media and ministry publicity.

Administer social media accounts for the church's special needs ministry.

Receive ministry participants at the special needs reception desk. Note changes that may potentially affect students' church experience.

Perform data input for new and updated participants' intake forms.

Assist with volunteer training event preparation.

Put on a puppet show related to the weekly Bible stories with help from student puppeteers.

Coordinate a service activity involving participants in the ministry (e.g., food drive).

Donate snacks, crafts, classroom equipment, music aids, and other requested items.

Plan and host a fun activity or respite event for ministry participants, siblings, and families.

- Skit Night or Talent Show
- Family Easter Egg Hunt
- Bowling Night
- Puppets and Popcorn
- Pools and Popsicles
- Movie Night and Crafts
- '50s Dress-up and Sock Hop
- Museum Tour
- Christmas Banquet
- Picnic at the Park
- Dress-up or Character Costume Party
- Service Project

Appendix 8.1
Inclusion Tips and Behavior Management Strategies

Create a Sensory Bin

Offer a self-contained scavenger hunt by hiding items related to the day's Bible story in a bin of dried beans or rice. Children who crave sensory input may also enjoy "fishing" for portions of a printed Bible verse, concealed inside of plastic eggs that are hidden in the bin. Students can then de-scramble the discovered printouts to make the day's Bible verse.

Allow Independent Time and Space

Often, children intuitively separate themselves from areas of over-stimulation or perceived disorganization. To see a table with a lot of choices for craft pieces and where a lot of other hands reach in may be overwhelming to a child with special needs. If a child walks away from an activity center, opting to play independently, they may be managing their own anxiety or calming themselves down.

Provide a Tangible Item to Hold During Story Time

Children will often absorb more teaching if they have something in their hands. How often do we notice adults doodling with a pen or playing with jewelry during the pastor's message? If you are a doodler, you know that keeping your hands busy in the midst of worship does not necessarily mean you aren't listening attentively. The same thing holds true for children with sensory needs. When possible, allow children to hold and play with an object that ties to the day's lesson during story time.

Define Personal Space at Activity Tables

Some children with special needs struggle with the concept of boundaries and space. Providing visual borders by using placemats and painters tape can promote better behavior. Boundaries may help a child understand where their portion of snacks or allotted craft pieces begin and end.

Provide Transition Aids

Cause-and-effect toys, such as a light-up spinning wand or a toy that plays music when you press a button may provide a managed distraction to a child who struggles with transitions. Giving a student something to focus on other than the move itself may help a child safely travel from one environment to the next. Guide ropes can also be effective tools even for children who may seem too old for such help.

Use Sounds and Music to Signal an Upcoming Activity

We've all heard the clean-up song used as a teacher's way of encouraging class cooperation to tidy up a room. But for many kids with special needs, having a specific song or sound to associate with an activity can be very helpful. Find a unique song or sound (e.g., chime of a bell) to consistently play to signal an upcoming transition or to indicate the need for students to do a particular task.

Provide Controlled Choices

Give children two or three options that are all acceptable to the group leader or buddy. For example, a student may be given the option of working on a craft alone, with a peer partner, or with their buddy. Or in another case the child may be given a choice of where they will sit in the room during the small group lesson or exercise. By pre-selecting and presenting a student with two or three acceptable choices, the child has the opportunity to feel in control inside their environment.

Provide a Quiet Corner

Set up an inexpensive pop-up tent, throw out a few comfy pillows, and place a beanbag in a slightly sequestered part of a room. When a child needs a moment to recollect and perhaps recover from overstimulation, offer the child a chill-out break. So often, undesirable behavior is an indicator that a child needs help with self-regulation. Do not view or present this chill-out option as a "time-out" punishment. Instead, offer positive praise when kids recognize and honor their need for downtime.

One interviewed teacher shared that she used a wagon with a built-in canopy instead of a tent. When a child was sitting inside the enclosed wagon, she could still see what was going on. Inside the wagon, the teacher placed pillows and soft blankets that were easy to wash. The teacher referred to the enclosed wagon as "Australia," which was a reference to the popular children's book *Alexander and the Terrible, Horrible, No Good, Very Bad Day* by Judith Viorst. And so it became popular to say that a participant needed to go to Australia. After a few minutes in the wagon the other peers would welcome a returning child back into the class. By referring to the quiet space with a clever name, the teacher had normalized the need for periodic visits to the quiet space.

Proactively Praise Kids

Whenever a child is observed making a good communication choice, make a point to offer praise. For a period of time, a small group leader or buddy may offer the child a sticker, or hand out a reward chip when a child raises his hand or makes a request (rather than blurting out a request or perhaps even hitting their neighbor). Finding ways to reinforce positive behavior may help to establish new patterns of communicating, especially for kids who struggle with good behavior choices.

Provide Visual Cues to Stop Undesirable Behavior

Each summer, I lead an age group for Vacation Bible School. Corralling a large number of energetic kids can be challenging, especially without constantly raising your voice. One summer, I kept a gigantic sombrero dangling off my neck and resting on my back. Whenever I desired a reduced noise level or needed the kids' attention, I quietly placed the sombrero on my head. Without having to yell or issue a negative-sounding demand, they responded beautifully. This strategy also works well for kids who don't receive or respond well to verbal instruction. Another trick is to keep a hand puppet nearby and whenever you need to disrupt undesirable behavior or gain immediate attention, pop the puppet on your hand and begin talking in a false voice. I can't explain it, but oftentimes kids who ignore a teacher's voice will stop whatever they are doing and observe the puppet's instruction.

Post a Visual Schedule

Post a visual schedule and refer to it before transitioning from one activity to another. Place recognizable pictures representing the day's activities in chronological order (e.g., large group, craft, Bible story, playground, snacks, music, go home, etc.). For the child who struggles with change, help him prepare for the change and provide him control by inviting him to move a symbol from the activity the group is leaving and re-placing that symbol on the upcoming activity. For children known to struggle with transitions, be sure to specifically give them a one-minute or five-minute warning so they can finish up their task and get ready for the next activity. Preparing kids for change ultimately helps them reduce anxiety.

Display Classroom Rules

Display short and concise rules with visual images to represent behavior reminders. Be sure to show corresponding pictures depicting realistic images for both the appropriate and desirable behaviors as well as inappropriate or undesirable behaviors. It is important to show and remind kids what you want them to do rather than just what you don't want them to do.

For example:

Use inside voice. Do not yell.

Respect your friends. Do not hit, push, or kick others.

Walk from place to place in line. Do not run away from the teacher or the class.

When I post classroom rules with pictures, I have a column on one side of the rules with a "Yes" header and then a column on the right with a "No" header. The "Yes" header has a green border or background and the "No" header has a red border or background. The corresponding pictures are then provided with a red or green border. For example, a picture of good behavior is bordered with green paper undesirable behavior is bordered in red paper.

NOTES

Chapter 1

1. Dawson Memorial Baptist Church in Birmingham, Alabama, has one of the most effective "Cradle Care Ministries" for expectant and new parents that I've ever seen. The church uses the ministry as outreach in the community to draw in families who see how the church celebrates expectant parents and newborns. Through the use of lay leaders, a relationship is initiated as soon as an expectant mother contacts the church with her due date. For more details on the ministry, see this post on The Inclusive Church Blog: http://theinclusivechurch.wordpress.com/2011/10/19/creating-a-cradle-care-ministry.

Chapter 2

1. http://www.cdc.gov/nchs/data/nhsr/nhsr065.pdf

2. http://www.nimh.gov/science-news/2013/study-documents-that-some-children-lose-autism-diagnosis.shtml

3. http://www.NewScientist.com/article/dn16941-savant-skills-may-be-widespread-in-people-with-autism.html

Introduction to Section 2

1. Megachurch is defined as a Protestant church with an average weekly attendance of more than 2,000 people. http://hirr.hartsem.edu/megachurch/definition.html

2. http://www.ScientificAmerican.com/article.cfm?id=autism-clusters-california-highly-educated-parents

3. http://www.cdc.gov/Features/CountingAutism

4. http://www.Guardian.co.uk/society/2012/dec/05/survival-rates-premature-babies-rise

5. http://HealthLand.time.com/2012/12/05/more-babies-are-surviving-extreme-preterm-birth-but-health-disabilties-remain

6. U.S. Department of Health & Human Services; Adopted Children with Special Healthcare Needs: Characteristics, Health, and Healthcare by Adoption Type, from the Assistant Secretary for Planning and Evaluation, October 2008, http://aspe.hhs.gov/hsp/08/cshcn/rb.shtml (from Table 3: Percent of Adopted Children with Special Health Care Needs (CSHCN) with Selected Adoption-Specific Characteristics, by Adoption Type).

Chapter 3

1. https://www.census.gov/newsroom/releases/archives/miscellaneous/cb12-134.html

2. http://www.cdc.gov/features/dsdev_disabilities/index.html

3. http://www.cdc.gov/ncbddd/developmentaldisabilities/features/birthdefects-dd-keyfindings.html

4. http://www.cdc.gov/mmwr/preview/mmwrhtml/ss6302a1.htm?s_cid=ss6302a1_w

5. Ibid.

6. http://www.cdc.gov/ncbddd/birthdefects/downsyndrome/data.html

7. http://www.cdc.gov/mmwr/preview/mmwrhtml/ss6302a1.htm?s_cid=ss6302a1_w

8. http://www.cdc.gov/ncbddd/adhd/features/key-findings-adhd72013.html

9. http://www.cdc.gov/ncbddd/developmentaldisabilities/features/birthdefects-dd-keyfindings.html

10. Ibid.

11. https://www.nidcd.nih.gov/about/congressional-justification-2015

12. https://www.census.gov/newsroom/releases/archives/miscellaneous/cb12-134.html

13. http://www.nimh.nih.gov/health/statistics/prevalence/any-anxiety-disorder-among-children.shtml

14. http://pedsinreview.aappublications.org/content/33/3/110.short

15. Adapted from: health.mo.gov/data/interventionmica/index_4.html

16. http://www.ncld.org/students-disabilities/iep-504-plan/what-is-iep

17. https://www.cde.state.co.us/cdesped/ssn

18. http://onlinelibrary.wiley.com/doi/10.1002/ajmg.c.31329/full

19. http://www2.ed.gov/about/offices/list/ocr/docs/hq9805.html

20. http://www.ada.gov/childq&a.htm

21. http://ada-il.org/questions/q_religious_orgs.php

22. http://www.universaldesign.com/index.php?option=com_content&view
=category&id=1695&itemid=488

23. Ibid.

24. http://designforall.org/en/dfa/dfa.php

Chapter 7

1. http://cdn.trustedpartner.com/docs/library/AchieveMCON2013/MIP_4Year
Summary_v2.pdf

2. To learn more about Stephen Ministries, visit https://www.stephenministries
.org.

3. For more information about Jim Wideman and his books, see www.
JimWideman.com.

4. http://www.onbeing.org/program/adam-grant-successful-givers-toxic-takers
-and-the-life-we-spend-at-work/transcript/8064#main_content

5. Erik W. Carter, *Including People with Disabilities in Faith Communities: A
Guide for Service Providers, Families, & Congregations* (Baltimore, MD: Paul H.
Brookes Publishing Co., 2007).

Chapter 8

1. http://www.nj.gov/education/students/safety/behavior/codes

2. See "Code of Student Conduct Compliance Checklist" at http://www.state
.nj.us/education/students/safety/behavior/codes/checklist.pdf.

3. www.ada.gov/childq&a.htm, U.S. Department of Justice, Civil Rights
Division Disability Rights Section, "Commonly Asked Questions about Child
Care Centers and The Americans with Disabilities Act." General Information: 3.

4. U.S. Department of Education, Office of Special Education Programs.
IDEA Regulations: Discipline 10.05.06—Page 1.

5. Ibid.

Chapter 10

1. http://pediatrics.aappublications.org/content/early/2014/08/12/peds.2014-
0594.abstract

2. http://www.cdc.gov/ncbddd/autism/data.html

3. Ibid.

4. http://www.ncbi.nlm.nih.gov/pmc/articles/PMC3162631

5. Based on "Refusing to Ignore Teenagers with Special Needs: Five Ideas for
Inclusion," originally published with Fuller Youth Institute, September 15, 2014,
http://fulleryouthinstitute.org/articles/special needs.

Appendix 7.1

1. http://www.childwelfare.gov/can/statistics/stat_disabilities.cfm
2. http://www.childwelfare.gov/responding/mandated.cfm

ABOUT THE AUTHOR

Amy Fenton Lee, who in a previous life, was a certified public accountant for a Big Four accounting firm, has written extensively on the subject of special needs inclusion, and blogs at www.theinclusivechurch.com. Amy grew up in the church as a "PK" (Preacher's Kid) and has since served as a volunteer leader in virtually every type of children's and preschool ministry environment. Amy lives in Atlanta with her husband and son.